Mysteries
of the Bush

PAIGE PATTERSON
and
ARMOUR

Scripture quotations taken from the New American Standard Bible®, Copyright © 1960, 1962, 1963, 1968, 1971, 1972, 1973, 1975, 1977, 1995 by The Lockman Foundation. Used by permission. (www.Lockman.org)

Seminary Hill Press
2001 West Seminary Drive
Fort Worth, Texas 76115

Mysteries of the Bush
By Armour Patterson, Paige Patterson
Copyright © 2015 by Armour Patterson, Paige Patterson
ISBN: 978-0-9839392-8-3
Publication Date: December 2015

CONTENTS

Preface	3
Chapter 1: Anticipating the Unexpected	9
Chapter 2: Turning the Hearts and Securing the Bonds	35
Chapter 3: The Glory of Young Men	53
Chapter 4: Hunting and Life	73
Chapter 5: The Harvest	117
Chapter 6: The Spirit, the Soul, and the Silent Places	137
Interlude: From the Land to the Waters	157
Chapter 9: The Bounty	183
Chapter 10: From Fishermen to Fishers of Men	193
Chapter 11: What to Do on an Expedition with a Boy	213
Chapter 12: Why Boys Need a Father	221
Chapter 13: A Church for Men Is a Church for All	227
Afterword	241

PREFACE

"Dad, if we go, can we hunt Africa?" This question from the lips of Armour, my 16-year-old son opened the curtains on an adventure more exciting than the dawning of the race to space. Webb Carroll, a faithful missionary, called me moments after Idi Amin was forced out of Uganda. "Dr. Patterson, I apologize for the short notice but I need two basketball teams of Christian high school and college students, and I need them tomorrow. Amin has left homeless, fatherless boys everywhere; and if we get to them now, we can help those boys to have a full and meaningful life, restore what the locusts have eaten, and introduce them to Christ."

We did not make "tomorrow," but a few months later we were there. Hundreds came to Christ; and our boys literally gave those African lads the shirts off their backs, the shoes off their feet, and the love of their hearts. All the boys were sick at some point during our six-week stay, but they played gamely on in the teaching sessions. If their parents had harbored the slightest idea of the danger to their sons from sporadic gunfire every day, I would have returned to a lynch mob stateside. The boys loved every minute. As one 19-year-old said, "This is the first and only really significant thing that I have done!"

Joe Barrow and Larry Scales, were missionaries in Tanzania. I had written Joe to see whether or not we could bring him any supplies. In 1984, missionaries made many sacrifices between stateside visits. Joe responded immediately with a list and with an invitation. "I have to fill all the deepfreezes at the seminary in Arusha so that the students can eat this year. I could use some help from you and Armour. What an answer to prayer! How about hunting wild game in Tanzania? Come on."

With snowcapped Mount Kilimanjaro overseeing our advance, we soon located beautiful Grant's Gazelles. The open plain provided almost no stealth options. A good 400 yards away several magnificent bucks were grazing. "Let's see if we can get closer," Joe opined. Boom! In far West Texas, Amour had already learned to make those long shots, and he wasn't about to risk losing this opportunity. "Unbelievable shot," Joe intoned. "How did that kid learn to shoot like that?"

That shot not only produced Armour's first African trophy (many more to come); but also, after field dressing the animal with uncanny dexterity, he looked wistfully up at Mount Kilimanjaro, observed the beauty of the wild terrain and finally observed, "I love you, Dad." A negative event of cataclysmic proportions could never separate that boy from his dad. His dad is a horribly imperfect man who has made his share of mistakes rearing his children, but that moment and a hundred more like it created a bond of steel impervious to life's vicissitudes.

So this book is about hunting. No, this book is about life—and eternity. This book is about how to get your son to heaven someday. Along the way you want your boy to handle the sorrows of life without turning to crime, bitterness, or suicide. You deeply desire for him to have those life values, which, unlike materialistic values, will endure and make him a real man. Your hope is that he will grow up to be an unselfish husband to his wife, an example to his own children, and a generous contributor to his world, which is the subject matter of this book. Father and son combine their narratives here—stories and philosophies laced with cogent insights from God's Word to bring you counsel that you will almost never read from today's painfully failed and feminized social agenda magnates.

Preface

Not every boy has a proclivity for the out-of-doors, for fishing and hunting. But every boy, regardless of interests, needs a dad who is a major participant, an encourager, and a counselor in his world—if that is the cyber world, orchestra, literature, or whatever—a dad who cares and gives himself to the child. Our world is the outdoor cosmos—room for all.

So sit with us on the rim of Ngorongoro Crater as the sun sets in the west, silhouetting the acacia trees and a herd of contentedly grazing buffalo and experience the awe and grandeur of our God. Weep with us at the grave of departed canine friend. Laugh until you cannot right yourself at the mockery of nature and the quagmires in which men immerse themselves. And learn the love of a father for a son and a son for a father.

ARMOUR
High Desert
Kingman, Arizona

and

PAIGE PATTERSON
Southwestern Baptist Theological Seminary
Fort Worth, Texas

CHAPTER 1

ANTICIPATING THE UNEXPECTED

Then Joseph could not control himself before all those who stood by him, and he cried, "Have everyone go out from me." So there was no man with him when Joseph made himself known to his brothers. ² He wept so loudly that the Egyptians heard it, and the household of Pharaoh heard of it. ³ Then Joseph said to his brothers, "I am Joseph! Is my father still alive?" But his brothers could not answer him, for they were dismayed at his presence.⁴ Then Joseph said to his brothers, "Please come closer to me." And they came closer. And he said, "I am your brother Joseph, whom you sold into Egypt. ⁵ Now do not be grieved or angry with yourselves, because you sold me here, for God sent me before you to preserve life. ⁶ For the famine has been in the land these two years, and there are still five years in which there will be neither plowing nor harvesting. ⁷ God sent me before you to preserve for you a remnant in the earth, and to keep you alive by a great deliverance. ⁸ Now, therefore, it was not you who sent me here, but God; and He has made me a father to Pharaoh and lord of all his household and ruler over all the land of Egypt.
Genesis 45:1-8

On a cool morning in the Land of Promise when Joseph, upon the mandate of his father, began his journey to find his herdsmen brothers at Dothan to ascertain their well-being, he had no clue how far this journey would take him. Sold by his brothers into slavery, taken to Egypt against his will, Joseph encountered every unexpected dilemma a man could imagine. Most common men would have despaired, imbibed legal and illegal drugs, sought solace in alcohol, or eventually ended the sad saga with suicide. But Joseph was not a common man. He was uncommon because his faith, in the providence of an all-knowing, just, and loving God, would not be shaken by things that happened along the way. In the end, he saved the lives of his brothers who wanted him out of their lives, and he rescued their families as well.

As many hunts and fishing expeditions as we have been privileged to enjoy, one single factor has always been the case: No journey into the wild ever turned out as it was intended. But from this fact emerges one of the most important lessons a father can impart to his son: Anticipate the unexpected, do the right thing, and always trust God. Learning to trust God in every exigency of life is among the most important peace-giving lessons for men in any era.

An Unanticipated Hunt

Some years ago I received a call from Richard Headrick, who, together with his wife Gina, was employed by Southeastern Baptist Theological Seminary where I was president. A sweet deal for the seminary—Headrick paid his own salary and expenses, gave additional money to fund the seminary, and visited all of our "2+2 Program" students, most of whom were serving in the most difficult and challenging fields in the world. They had two strategic assignments. First, they encouraged these students; and second, they evaluated their progress in the work. The Headricks were perfect for both assignments, but sometimes I got more than I anticipated. Such was the case on the day I took this call.

Anticipating the Unexpected

"Hey, Dr. Patterson, we just got back from Spruceland (you will not find this in an atlas as I manufactured the name to protect the work). Fred Osiander (also pseudonym) and his wife are in a remote valley and have made friends with the prince (he really was not, but he did rule the valley), who is an avid hunter. He told him about you, and the man thinks that you are *bwana*[1] from Africa. He wants to hunt with you in Spruceland, and Fred thinks that if you will do it, the prince is open to the Lord."

Now I know all about Spruceland, and the thought of hunting there had all the appeal of a trip to visit my local mortician, which is exactly where I figured this journey would terminate. But I could not disappoint my student. And besides, if there were any chance that the prince would find the Lord, I had to do it. Besides, in the mountains of Spruceland, there was some really great game.

A flight into the capital of Spruceland on a real plane was followed by an exciting flight (one way to put it) on Spruceland Air to an interior town unknown to me. This was followed by a three-hour car ride, which began on a gravel road, soon giving way to dirt roads harboring canyons that appeared to be as precipitous and deep as the Grand Canyon. Arriving in the valley hideaway, otherwise known as a town, we met the prince and his delightful family. What wonderful people! And how proud I was of my student!

The hunt was not what I was expecting. A two-hour drive into the "back country" (remember where we were) brought us to the hunting grounds. Here we made the acquaintance of the hunting party—all 120 of them! If that were not shock enough, they—all armed with AK-47s—arrived in the back of one huge truck. The hunting technique was as unique as its participants. Making an enormous circle, probably 300

---

[1] Swahili word for "master" or "boss," used as a form of respectful address in parts of Africa.

yards from one side to the other, the hunting dogs were loosed to run through no-man's land chasing out deer and pig. Of course, the noise of arriving hunters guaranteed that all self-respecting game in the area had already vacated, but that did not prevent the hunters from free-fire at any movement.

Beneath a tree, Headrick, Osiander, and I dug in as deeply as we could. Tree limbs torn loose by errant AK-47 fire showered us. I looked at Headrick and Osiander and said something like, "In the unlikely scenario that we come out of here alive, I am going to shoot you both in a kind, gentle manner and send you on to heaven." They laughed, and finally I laughed.

We were all rejoicing when rest time arrived. Shooting stopped, and we assembled. Each of us was presented a large bowl of water buffalo butter. Then someone came by with fresh, wild honey and doused each mound of butter. Flat bread arrived, and we learned to dip it in the concoction. Best thing I ever ate! But it was the prelude to the next disaster. Water buffalo butter is like a two-month sojourn in the Empty Quarter of Saudi Arabia. I have never been that thirsty! And in a further effort to streamline my mortality, nobody brought any bottled water!

Always insanely optimistic, Richard said that a well nearby would be safe—this information from the same man who proposed the whole adventure. The problem of the well's content—which I figured included typhus, typhoid fever, and dysentery: There was only one cup, and we were the last to the well. There was no good choice, only a question of how you wished to die. We chose not to die of thirst, and I write this today as a testament to the grace of God.

Next, the men announced a shooting match with pistols. Headrick, the coward, disappeared along with my student. Pistols were old, rusty, and virtually inoperative. The clay pot 50 feet away may as well have contained afternoon tea. It was totally safe. No one came close. "Your turn, Bwana" (that's I), someone said. Now I am no marksman. Any prowess I have is with a rifle. I do fine with pistols, but I knew from what I had observed that there was little hope to hit any target with their pistols. But I also knew that it was important to our mission for me to destroy that clay pot. I noticed that one young man had a reasonably new semi-automatic with some store-bought ammo. I agreed to shoot if he would place his pistol on loan to me. Then I silently prayed. I knew God could care less who prevails in a shooting contest, but I felt certain that he understood Bwana's predicament.

I prepared to shoot during the only time all day when quiet reigned—the quiet of a tomb! I prayed diligently. "Oh, dear Lord, hold my hand steady. Make my aim true. Guide this bullet in a trajectory of witness." Boom! As pieces of clay flew in all directions, a mighty cheer ascended. Now the door was open to tell them of the love of Christ. With Bwana talking, they would listen. But Bwana knows that he almost certainly could have emptied that clip without another hit!

Well, the wildlife of Spruceland was undisturbed. The only victim was one dog, and that was by an AK-47 round through the ear, so it was not fatal. It did precipitate an argument over who hit the unfortunate canine—a futile argument with so many projectiles in the air. But I felt as though it was not a wholesome debate with 100-plus guns in the arena. That, by the grace of God, ended the scariest hunt of my life. Would I do it again? You bet, I would do it for the adventure alone, but some did receive Christ, and that turned Spruceland into paradise. None of this could have been predicted, but the providence of God prevailed.

Unanticipated Armament

Some folks think that unexpected hunts deserve unanticipated armament. Southwestern Seminary Chaplain Dean Nichols never realized the events he set in place. In 1999 and 2000, I was twice elected president of the Southern Baptist Convention. Given the fact that I had, since 1979 been the chief troublemaker in the SBC, this was an honor totally unexpected. Alaskan pastor Dean Nichols, later chaplain of Southwestern Seminary, wanted to do something to express gratitude for what I had encountered from 1979 to 2000 during the years of upheaval in the Southern Baptist Convention. Knowing my love for Africa and the hunt and having heard me talk about the thrill of shooting the ultimate elephant rifle—a .500, he decided to purchase the rifle for me from Krieghoff in Germany. "$28,000! You have to be prevaricating," Nichols shouted. He could not have put together $28.00 on his Alaskan pastor's salary.

Then he had an idea. How many would give $100? He found enough. Some gave more. Dean gave out of his generosity far more than he should have. One or two pledged and never gave. Somehow it came together. The convention was meeting in Atlanta, and by this time my son Armour was deeply involved. Insofar as anyone knows, no one in the world ever was wounded or killed by a shot from a .500. At $28,000, you do not have them being passed around the neighborhood. But two preachers, one a pastor and the other an evangelist, protested the presentation of the rifle on the floor of the convention. Had I known, I would have overruled their objection, but it was a surprise. Had they given me an automobile, it would have been fine, even though more people are killed every year by automobiles than by guns, let alone by .500s. The two preachers were the unfortunate victims of left-wing politics!

What a nice gift! And the rifle has saved my life now three times. I have taken two Cape buffalo, fired the final shot on a lion, an Alaskan brown bear, a large hippopotamus, and a crocodile. I have hunted elephant (out of my price range now), and a number of other animals, including a puff adder. I admit that in the last case it was overkill, but I do not really care for those ambush-inclined reptiles.

Dean Nichols himself got to use it in hunting Rick McCrary's hippo and some other quarry. In fact, he was racking up the whole South African countryside when he got a chance for a beautiful greater kudu with its long spiral horns. Excited, he took a fine bead (something you do not do with a rifle for dangerous game) and squeezed off a round. "How did I miss?" he said, looking askance at the rifle. The second shot had the same effect except the kudu decided to start moving. While Dean examined the rifle, I handed him two more bullets. "Load," I said as forcibly as I knew how. Obediently, he complied, and this time completed a very hard shot. The end result is one of the prettiest kudus I ever saw now on the chaplain's wall.

Unforgettable Creatures

That leads me to the question of what to do with the animals that you take. Much of what the American hunter takes is for meat. But when you take a really nice animal, why not have the taxidermist do a really nice, even creative, mount? Then, do not keep it to yourself, but use it as an educational mount for children. Hundreds every year visit the Chicago Museum of Natural History to see the two Tsavo lions that killed 162 workmen and shut down the building of the Kenyan Railway until non-hunter, engineer John Henry Patterson—despite making enough beginner blunders to have been victim #163—finally took both lions. Not what he signed on for.[2]

A steady parade of families with children and classes from various schools drop by my office at the seminary to see my fifty-plus mounts. Quite an education to be up close to animals they know but also

---

2 John Henry Patterson, *The Man-Eaters of Tsavo* (Guilford, CT: The Lyons Press, 2004).

to learn about the gorgeous, fully mounted nyala, the puku, the Lichtenstein's hartebeest, the tsessebe, roan, and the oribi. They see a baboon reading Darwin's *Origin of the Species* and observe a North Carolina taxidermist's mount of a male and female cape buffalo that look so real you almost need a weapon in hand to look. Needless to say, the baboon provides me the opportunity to spell out Darwin's mistakes and say a word for the Creator.

Mark Howell, my son-in-law, who serves as pastor of First Baptist Church in Daytona Beach, Florida, has hunted Africa as well. Has God blessed this man? In his office are two animals in the top twenty-five of all ever taken! See his red hartebeest and his recently harvested puku. What unbelievably magnificent animals. Born in a Pennsylvania city, Mark never anticipated this turn in his life. Son Armour and daughter-in-law Rachel have a small home in Melissa, Texas; but if you go through, do not miss it, and be sure you invite yourself to supper because few prepare fish and game with the culinary expertise of this man. Even in that small home, they have quite a collection, including Armour's fabulous kudu and Rachel's beautiful zebra just taken in Zambia.

All of this is mentioned just to say: Use your trophies to teach about the animals and also to talk about the things of God. And speaking of taxidermy, are you looking for a profession? Taxidermists usually run nine months to a year behind because there is more work than there are taxidermists. If you have a flair for art and love for animals, you can do quite well in taxidermy. Our seminary owns a beautiful painting of a duggaboy, the old lone cape buffalo bull painted on a canvas of buffalo hide. The bottom of the hide extends beyond the painting in an imaginative flair of South African artist Kobus Möller. Every year at Safari Club International, the wildlife exhibits are unforgettable, but the exquisite wildlife art is among the finest anywhere.

Finding Humor in the Unexpected

Near-Disaster

If you hunt, you are sure to face some interesting moments. One of the most effective ways to hunt brown bear in Alaska is from tree stands, but that has its own challenges. First, the brown bear, due to the construction of the bony sections around his shoulders, and due to his weight, cannot climb trees. Black bears can and do, and that's a story of its own. But if a brown bear can't climb a tree, he can shake one of almost any size and has been known to shake hunters out of trees. So, therefore, we have looked for very sturdy trees from which we were reasonably sure we could not be shaken out. Pastor Dean Nichols noted that the tree stand needed to be pretty high, so it was placed about 30 to 40 feet above ground. For a large man like yours truly, it was quite a climb to get up to the old tree stand, which was comprised of nothing more than a canvas seat. Pastor Nichols did not tell me that the canvas seat was just about as old as I (understand "ancient") and in that condition was certainly not a good holding place for a 220-pound man. Getting into his tree stand, located some feet behind him, Nichols watched as I climbed with care into my own. The problem came the second I sat down. The old canvas material had rotted, and the sound of the rip was second only to the fear and sense of falling. Now you probably would never believe that an old 220-pound codger could make a pirouette in thin air and somehow end up in a hugging relationship with the tree. But the problem is that the 30-foot fall would certainly have taken me out of any future hunts, so there was no alternative.

Now in this one case there was genuine concern in Pastor Nichols' heart. The moment when I started my descent, it occurred to Pastor Nichols that he would have to explain to Mrs. Patterson that I had met my demise on his watch. So, for a brief second, he was actually concerned. Then he saw me clinging desperately to the tree and nearly killed himself laughing from his own tree stand. In fact, he was so amused that he never got around to assisting me, but I finally made it to the steps and got myself down from the tree—shaken, but happy to be alive. We all enjoyed a considerable laugh and got back to hunting. However, I did not forget the incident.

Payback

A few days later, we were in a different part of the Alaskan outback. Once again, stationed in tree stands, Dean Nichols was a few feet ahead of me with his back turned to my position so that we could watch in both directions. We sat there for what seemed like forever. We were treated to quite a show by a black bear that came out and rolled around the ground and scratched his back on a tree. At that point he saw me, came over, and looked up in the tree. As a matter of fact, he decided to come up and investigate what this strange form of life might be. This action was unfortunate, not because I was in any danger but because I had already taken all the black bear I wanted or needed, and I really didn't want to have to shoot this one. The black bear came right on up the tree until he got to the point where his next reach would have been my foot. I had my .454 Cassul pointed right between his eyes, and I kept shouting at the bear to go down. Finally, he must have been persuaded by the length of the barrel or the size of the hole in the bore of the pistol—he went back down and sauntered off into the forest. So much for the adventure for the day!

After six hours in the tree, Pastor Nichols asked forgiveness but said, "I just have to take care the urges of life." So I said, "Don't bother about me." He stood in his tree stand and took care of his business.

However, I had noticed that right next to me was one of the aspen trees with the unusual bark that tears away from the trunk of the tree. As Pastor Nichols sat down, I simply grabbed a piece of the loose bark and ripped it from the tree. He thought the canvas of his seat was ripping like mine had done a few days before and leaped back to attention, almost taking himself out of the tree. For just a moment I was afraid my prank had gone too far. Once I saw that he was stabilized in his tree stand and was looking back at me with his heart pumping, I began to laugh. I then called his attention to what had happened a few days before and explained that it was simply time to get even. Safe at last, he, too, had a good laugh. Laughter is important when you are hunting. If you cannot laugh at the unexpected disasters of the hunt, you will be ill-equipped for life.

Monkeyshines

Late one evening in Alaska, we had been hunting brown bear. We had not yet gotten a good look at one, but we knew that they were nearby because they are not silent creatures. Large-boned and heavy, they can be heard all around you. On top of that, they make no effort to conceal their grunts since they have no natural enemies other than man and are quite unafraid of most things. It had been getting dark for two hours and was getting progressively darker. Those on the four-wheelers who were supposed to come and fetch us to camp, for whatever reason, had not materialized. Although we were well-armed—Nichols with a .458 and Patterson with a .500 double rifle—it occurred to us that we were having less and less vision as the night darkened. We decided to retreat all the way to the large river where we knew we would be safe from at least one direction and where we would only have to watch one direction with some peripheral vision in either of the other two possible directions. The river at this point was nearly a half-mile wide, so we had no problems there. A brown bear can certainly cross it, but you would be able to hear him coming from quite some distance.

At this point, again, Pastor Nichols said, "I need to relieve myself. Can you watch for just a second?" He leaned his rifle against a bush. He turned to the river, and I waited until he was just about half through meeting nature's demand. Then I shouted, "Here he is, Dean! It's show time!" At that same moment I shouldered my rifle and acted as though a brown bear was on us. The flurry of activity immediately behind me was amazing to behold. Somehow Pastor Nichols grabbed his rifle and got into a shooting position. The problem was, of course, that he had not completed the other business that he had begun. In fact, the whole situation may have resulted in a proliferation of that first activity. Needless to say, he was not particularly happy about it until he discovered that there actually was no bear, at which point he began to laugh at the circumstance. Perhaps you can understand why the Alaskan guide finally said that he was not going to hunt anymore with both of us together. He said, "You two guys have too much fun, but in the doing of it you make too much noise, and we never will get a brown bear." He separated us, and sure enough, within a day or two I had an opportunity to take my brown bear.

Adrenaline Junkie

Traveling high on top of the Land Rover, armed with a .308, we were hunting smaller antelopes to set up bait for lions. Suddenly, I was nearly launched by the uncharacteristically abrupt stop. Straining to see the cause of the braking, our tracker pointed to the two-o'clock position. "Biggest lion we have seen out here in years," he said. "But do you want a female?" Finally focusing on the 420-pound lioness eating her morning antelope breakfast, I observed, "She is beautiful." We moved up slowly. About 300 yards away, she became nervous and moved to the bush, turning and facing us. "Please make a good shot," said the professional hunter. "Too many people out here to have an angry, wounded kitty." When the round flew from the bore of the rifle, the lioness leaped into the air, roared so ferociously that my wife heard her in the camp two miles away. Into the bush darted a wounded lion.

What happens next is a military operation. Walking point with a tracker on either side watching the blood trail, I advanced, rifle on shoulder, safety disengaged. The hunter's eyes are straight ahead in the tall grass. A professional hunter was 30 yards on either side in case the lion circled. Suddenly the trackers ran. They saw her perfectly camouflaged in the grass. Even had I seen her, there was no shot available, but when they ran, she sprang as they anticipated. Now she lay at my feet, inches away in all her regal beauty. Now in full mount she adorns my office. But if you are an adrenaline junkie, there is nothing to match that moment.

Exceptional Picnic

Non-hunters can enjoy the journey also. Mrs. Patterson's idea of "suffering for Jesus" is a really nice Marriott. But being a trooper of German-Irish descent, she has made every African safari except one. While she does not hunt, she takes great pictures and within minutes of arriving is the general of the camp. What she really loves is British high tea. So as a trade-off, our entire family has become a family of exotic tea drinkers. Even Chayil, my black Labrador retriever, will awake with a bolt from an afternoon siesta at the sound of a teacup or the words "tea time." He is not into Earl Grey, but he loves the scones and Devonshire Cream.

So imagine my surprise when, on a visit to my son in Arizona, Armour announced that we would be going that afternoon for British high tea. In Arizona? Where? In the Cochise Mountains, of course. Well, why didn't I think of that? Frankly, I simply could not get the whole thing to make a bit of sense, especially when we put the Treeing Walker Coonhound in the back of the truck. But we all boarded the pickup as ordered and drove into the mountain hideout where Cochise eluded the U.S. Cavalry for his entire life. Tea time? Where?

Finding a lonely ridge overlooking the mountain forest, Armour parked the truck. He then unveiled camp chairs, which he placed in the bed of the pickup. While Bandit (the dog) sniffed every mountain scent, Armour made a fire and boiled the water for the tea. Fresh sandwiches, followed by recently baked scones with real Devonshire Cream and jam were placed before us on the small table in the bed of the vehicle. From that indescribably beautiful scene, we watched a magnificent sunset, augmented by the occasional fox or deer run out by Bandit. We even enjoyed a concert of priceless music chosen by Armour and accompanied by Bandit. Whenever that hound heard music (often around our place) he would make a trumpet out of his mouth, look heavenward, and bay at the top of his lungs in amazing syncopation with the music and most of the time in tune.

At the end of the day, even Mama had to admit that this was the most opulent tea she had ever witnessed. This was just one of the precious, unexpected family memories that every family ought to experience. Mama even said that it was better than the Dorchester in London!

Opportunities

One of the most unexpected turns in any hunt is the opportunity to say a word for Jesus. My son-in-law Mark Howell came from a nominally Christian family but was quite confident that neither his mom nor dad knew the Lord. We all began to pray that God would give an understanding of the gospel to both Larry and Donna, and we looked for opportunities to share the gospel with them. Mark observed one day that his dad loved to hunt and would love to see our west Texas playground. I thought that was a great idea, so we invited him to go with us to the ranch where we hunted in west Texas. One day, Armour and Mark had to chase a deer far down into the canyon, leaving Larry alone with me on top. We were there for a couple of hours together.

Anticipating the Unexpected

I had my first opportunity to share the gospel with Mark's father. I believe that Larry came to understand what it was all about on that occasion. Later he actually trusted the Lord. Mark had the opportunity to baptize his own father. Likewise, his mother came to the Lord, and we rejoice in that whole family's salvation.

The point to be made here is that there is no better place for a born-again believer to take a lost man than on a hunt. There in the wilderness you will have the opportunity to share with him in a remarkable way, and God will bless that time of sharing the gospel. This is one of the unexpected blessings of the hunt.

Surprising Encounter

Adventure presents itself anywhere and everywhere. Traveling in Israel is not a place where most people would expect to find adventure. But if you get outside the city, adventure will often find you. Ein Gedi (the "well of the goat") is a beautiful vertical oasis that begins at the waters of the Dead Sea and runs straight up the side of the mountain into the wilderness of Judea. It is notable as the place where David hid from King Saul and could actually have taken Saul's life, but David said, "I will not lift up my hand against God's anointed" (1 Samuel 24:10). That's a good lesson for everyone to learn.

Ein Gedi is known as "the well of the goat" because of the beautiful ibex that frequent the surrounding wilderness. When you are climbing up to the waterfall, running across these beautiful animals is not at all uncommon. They love the precipitous cliffs of the Judean wilderness and survive magnificently there. If you keep going beyond the waterfall, you can make a hard climb all the way up to the top of the prominence and visit the ruins of a Chalcolithic temple. I have only done that one time, but it was memorable to a degree I had not anticipated. The climb is quite precipitous, and as I made my way up the ladder that had been nailed into the rock, I finally reached the top. As I pulled myself up onto the last rung of the ladder, I was face to face with a young leopard. I would say the leopard was about a year old and probably weighed in the neighborhood of 80 or 90 pounds. It is quite difficult to ascertain who was more surprised—the climber or the leopard. Needless to say, for the next century (probably 15 to 20 seconds), we stared at one another. I knew that it was best not to run, but there was really no possibility of that anyway. A slow retreat down the ominous ladder was about the only possibility, but there were people behind me. On the other hand, I had no real desire, possessing no weapon whatever, to contest the suzerainty of the leopard over the high rocks. We had heard that leopards had returned to the lands of the Bible. The Dead Sea Valley, where Ein Gedi is located, is a part of the Great Rift Valley, which comes all the way from Africa. That's why David encountered lions, leopards, and other African animals there in Israel.

Well, fortunately for me, that beautiful leopard—painted with the artistry of His maker—decided that too many people were invading the premises; he turned and ran. I breathed a sigh of relief, and we crawled on up to view the Chalcolithic temple.

Capricious Cat

Strangely enough for all of my opportunities to parley with leopards in Africa, I was never bitten by a leopard in Africa. I was not so fortunate in India. We had gone into one of the country's famous national parks, where there are tiger reserves, hoping to see some of those magnificent beasts. We never saw a tiger in the wild, but we did come across some remarkable sloth bears—an astonishment not only to us but also to the guides, who said they were seldom seen. We were able to view two of them for quite a while.

Anticipating the Unexpected

Our guide, having discovered that I loved animals, asked if I would like to see the leopard that they had found abandoned by its mother and were rearing in captivity. They were just about to turn him back out into the wild, but right now he was in a large cage. Of course I said I would love to see him. We traveled to an out-of-the-way ranger station, and in the large walk-in cage in the back was a beautiful year-old leopard probably weighing about 60 pounds. The park ranger asked if I would like to go into the cage with the leopard. Not thinking about much except the opportunity to be that close to one of these great cats, I assured him that I would be happy to go in with him. I was not to report this visit to anybody since it was not really allowed, and I agreed. Going into the enclosure, the playful leopard saw the ranger, his favorite toy, come in the gate and immediately launched a playful attack on the man, leaping up into his arms. I thought all of that looked like much fun, but when the young leopard got his teeth around the man's throat, I became concerned. I knew that the leopard was not going to hurt him intentionally, but a year-old leopard with his teeth firmly attached to the throat of the ranger was not what I had anticipated.

I could tell by the look of terror in the ranger's eye that he was less than ebullient about the whole matter himself. He had both hands on the leopard's sides and was attempting to pull him away. I decided that he needed help, so I reached over and took hold of the leopard around the top of his shoulders close to his neck. When I did so, the playful leopard turned and nipped at me. Again, there was no intention to do real harm, but to everybody's surprise, my hand began spurting blood into the air. I have a large vein that crosses the top of my hand, and the lucky cat had nipped a hole in that vein, and it looked like the Lucas Gusher in the oil fields of southeast Texas. I knew I wasn't hurt and wasn't concerned about the outcome. I was glad to get the cat off of the ranger, and we retreated to the opening. Now the ranger was stupendously concerned about me and how he would explain to his superiors why he had a bleeding client. Fortunately, we got through all the official nightmare, and I lived to tell about my encounter with the Indian leopard.

Incalculable Risks

Crocodile hunting sounds easy but usually proves to be much more difficult than it appears. The wily lizards, having survived from earliest times, may not be the smartest animals on the planet, but their instincts are good. Just about the time you get to where you can take a shot, suddenly the croc will make his move for the water, and you have missed your opportunity. I have had a number of interesting events happen while hunting crocs. Probably the one I remember the most vividly was crawling through heavy underbrush in perfect croc country looking for a specimen. I was a little uncomfortable in the heavy growth, much of which had fallen on the forest floor and now provided a cushion of about six inches. The reason for my discomfort was not so much the crocodiles but especially cobras and other snakes that like to be close to the water. I was lying in one position waiting to begin my crawl forward once again when I felt movement directly beneath my chest. Lifting myself up as gingerly as I could, I was startled to see, about three inches beneath me, a cobra moving across my path. I had felt his movement, and we were on much closer terms than I found comfortable. Grateful, however, for the heavy underbrush that kept him from getting in a striking position, I was able to make my retreat.

No Sure Shot

Later that same day, I had the heartbreaking experience that every hunter eventually has in Africa. Until that moment, I had never lost an animal, even with 18 forays into Africa. That circumstance has two great assets. First, even professional hunters have lost animals before,

Anticipating the Unexpected

and so you become a man of significant status if you have never lost an animal. Privately, however, I think that a good many of the trackers and professional hunters with whom we worked were looking forward to the day when I would lose an animal.

The second great advantage is that you don't have to pay for an animal that you do not hit. In Africa, if they know for certain that the animal has been wounded, then you pay for the animal whether you find him or not. On this particular day, we were able to get very close to a 14-foot croc. He was a beautiful green-and-yellow color, and I knew that he was definitely one that I wanted. One problem was that he was on a sandbar across about 25 feet of water and located about 100 yards away from where I was lying on the ground. It was worth the try. Commonly, people make the mistake of aiming for the heart shot or the shoulder of the croc. Unless the croc is far inland, that is not a high-percentage shot. Even if you make the fatal shot, the nervous system of the croc is so designed that he plunges into the water before he has an opportunity to die. Then things really get interesting. You can go in looking for the wounded and hopefully dead croc. However, this is a less than salubrious task because he has a number of other friends and relatives in the area, and this is to say nothing of the hippos that are normally omnipresent in such bodies of water.

There are two shots that are much more reliable. One is the brain shot. Unfortunately, the crocodile's brain is only about the size of a chicken egg, so it is a daunting shot to have to make. The better option is to come a hand's-length behind where his two jaws are hinged together. If you make that shot, you sever his spinal cord and therefore he will simply drop flat and will not make it to the water. That is what I intended to do on this particular croc. Fortunately, I apparently did make a really good shot, and the croc dropped and did not run for the water. However, one of the men with me was just sure that he might try to make it and decided to play the hero and ran toward the croc to try to keep him from getting into the water that divided us. With the croc's last energy, indicating that I had not actually severed the entire spinal column, somehow it got into the water. We worked for hours to try to find him, but it was futile. The African hunter had lost his first animal. That is expensive and hurts for a long time to come, but it is part of hunting and only made me more determined to get the nice crocodile that I was later able to take. Disappointment is an integral part of life. But it only destroys those whose spirits are unprepared for its inevitability.

Serious Persistence

A hunter must learn to be patient. Patience is one of the most important lessons to be learned from hunting, and it transfers instantly into everything else in the social order. On the hunt once again for a crocodile in South Africa, we heard that a very fine specimen had been seen in the Crocodile River south of the Kruger Game Park. So, early in the morning, we approached the spot. One thing I do not like about hunting in South Africa is the prevalence of fences. Zimbabwe, with the relative absence of those fences, makes a far preferable hunting ground, to my way of thinking. But we had to go in the gate here. As we went through the gate, I noticed that there were four ostriches. I could tell that they were the gatekeepers for the place because they eyed us with some suspicion. I was particularly aware of the beady eyes of one of those creatures that looked at us as if to say, "Ah, fresh prey today." So I warned everybody in our party, "Watch out for the ostriches." One might not think that an ostrich is particularly dangerous. The pecking of his beak is irritating but certainly not dangerous. What one has to watch are those feet. The middle claw on the ostrich is capable of eviscerating a man, and more than one man has died or been seriously injured as a result of such an attack.

Anticipating the Unexpected

The crocodile we found was a beauty and was involved in a cat-and-mouse game with a duck that he wanted to eat. The duck knew exactly what was in the crocodile's small mind. When the croc swam away from the edge and out into the middle of the water, the duck would get down into the water and entice the croc back. The croc would come cruising back, and the wise duck would jump out and run up the shore so that he was beyond the reach of the crocodile. This went on for a full four hours. Finally, the croc tired of the game, and we were grateful that our patience was rewarded. We watched as the croc went to one bank and partially crawled out.

Running around to the other side, I got positioned, ready to take a shot with my .300 Win Mag. The other people in the party were coming around to our side also. We had cautioned everybody to be very quiet and not disturb the croc. At that time I heard shouting and about the biggest commotion that I had ever heard. As Chaplain Dean Nichols and the professional hunter came around one edge of the water, they came face-to-face with the Gestapo, namely, the ostrich. Accordingly, he attacked Nichols. The bird towered over Nichols and proceeded to peck the top of his head. This is a painful but ultimately non-dangerous experience. Nichols, however, was getting enough of it. Every time he would try to stop the pecking by moving his rifle upward, he would remember the claws and then would drop the rifle back down. When he dropped the rifle down to protect himself from the claws, the bird resumed pecking his head. He was just about to turn around and shoot the bird when the professional hunter distracted the bird long enough for Nichols to be able to get by. So much for stealth in the hunt! The croc got back in the water and swam around for a while, and again we were compelled to wait. Finally, the croc emerged but totally across the lake where the river water had pooled. Although he crawled completely out onto the mud, he was now better than 100 yards away and so positioned that I could only make the brain shot. His head was farthest away from me and his tail closest to me.

To make matters infinitely worse, my own position was not a good one. We had crawled up on a large termite mound, and there was almost no place to stand. Certainly, I could not put one foot behind the other so that my feet were parallel to one another on what amounted to about a five-inch track on top of the termite mound. Below me there was an 8-foot drop with a number of smaller crocodiles lying on the shore. Behind me there was an approximately 16-foot drop, which at my age would not have been a good thing. The croc was still, so I had my opportunity, and I took aim. The professional hunter at the last moment said, "Dr. Patterson, I'd really rather you not take that shot." I thought that he had a question about whether or not I could hit the croc. I turned and looked at him and said, "Why don't you want me to take the shot?"

He said, "If you shoot and knock yourself off of the termite mound, I hate to think about having to pick up the pieces." He was kind enough not to refer to the age of the hunter, but I knew what he meant.

I replied, "I've been trying to get a croc for two years, and this is the best shot I've had. I'm going to take it."

"All right," he said, "I suppose that's the hunter's choice, but please be careful."

Boom! I hit the crocodile but about a half-inch to the right of his brain. It knocked him loopy, so he writhed but did not get into the water. Boom! This time I was about a half-inch to the left of the brain but with good effect. Still he moved. Boom! The final shot finished him off and was a perfect shot.

At the other end of the lake, the other professional hunter said to Chaplain Nichols, "My goodness, is that man using a machine gun?"

"No," the chaplain replied. "It's a bolt-action, but he was serious about getting his croc."

Apparently, they had never seen a bolt-action rifle used that quickly at that distance. In any event, thankfully today, I have a fabulous crocodile fully mounted in my office and a wonderful story of a police bird who arrested Chaplain Nichols.

Motion Picture Motivations

To whet your appetite for the African bush, let us do something that we don't usually do and recommend some movies for your consumption. Ghost in the Darkness is the story of the Tsavo lions that shut down the British railway. The story does not follow all points with the book, which is the accurate version written by the man named Patterson who actually killed the two lions. However, the movie itself does present to the viewer the pressure of African hunting. I recommend it but perhaps not to be watched at night before you try to sleep.

The series of movies about the Zulu nation is historically based and worth the time. The first movie *Shaka Zulu,* the second movie *Zulu*, and the third movie *Zulu Dawn* trace the history of the difficulties the Zulus faced with the British invading army. Once I had the opportunity to visit Isandlwana and the Buffalo River where the Brits, in the first case, were massacred and, in the second case, held out against insuperable odds and eventually were saluted by the Zulus for their courage. The insights (about life in Africa) gained from these movies are quite helpful in introducing the viewer to the Zulu nation, the most militant of all the African tribal people.

Another movie worth watching is *Out of Africa*, which has a great scene of a lion charge—as a matter of fact a charge from two lions. The whole scenario is one that could easily take place in Africa where there are lions.

No "Plan B"

Hunting is always challenging; but, by all rights, if you just want unbelievable adventure, the Cape buffalo hunt is still perhaps the finest of all endeavors. On my first Cape buffalo hunt, I was too slow in squeezing off a round. As I did so, a female walked right in front of the male. At least the shot was perfect, and something happened that seldom happens—the female Cape buffalo went down immediately. I was disappointed to have missed the male. Later, I was able to get a really beautiful classic male, and together they make a great mount in my office.

On this day, however, we were standing looking at the deceased female when all of a sudden we discovered the herd, which had run off, gotten angry, and returned. This was not unusual for Cape buffalo. We found ourselves standing and watching a line of some 60 Cape buffalo not more than 40 yards away. At first I wasn't concerned. Then I noticed that all the trackers had climbed trees. This was understandable since the trackers had no weapons, but it was also alarming because I knew that I would never be able to shimmy up the tree trunks where they had found refuge. This left me standing with two professional hunters, three rifles, and some 60 buffalo threatening to overrun us. One of the hunters began shouting at them. When he paused for just a few moments, I asked the logical question: "Anybody want to let me in on Plan A and Plan B?" I queried. "There is no Plan B, and Plan A is we have to get them to go away."

"And if they don't? And if they come, what do we do?" I asked with a certain amount of urgency.

"Well, here's what we will do," said the other professional hunter. "Focus all of our fire on the five or six that are coming in the middle and are closest to us. Try to take as many of them down as we can, and then, at the last moment, we're going to dive in—all three of us—right in at

Anticipating the Unexpected

the stomach of the fallen buffalo that you've already taken. Hopefully, they will run by us and not over us with animals on the ground."

"And will that work?" I asked.

"I have no idea," said the professional hunter. "I've never had to do it before."

Well, that was the most intense moment that I've experienced in buffalo hunting. I'm glad to say that we were finally able to persuade the buffalo to limit their casualties and ours and go away. We had a charge from the big male buffalo that I took at a later time, which made that hunt exciting; but I was able to get him on the ground when he was about 20 feet away. In a more recent Cape buffalo hunt, our hunters all had to climb termite mounds in order to avoid the charge of a buffalo. Pete Fisher, the outfitter in Zambia with whom we were hunting, had the experience of being chased around the tree repeatedly by a female buffalo with an unusually undeveloped sense of humor. Pete was glad to be alive when the whole thing was over. He was able to laugh about it by the time we got there, but it was no laughing matter at the time.

The Point

Few endeavors of life prepare a boy for the unexpected in this earthly journey like hunting and fishing. Here one learns patience, fear, disappointment, hurt, victory, exhilaration, triumph, and joy—sometimes all in a single morning. And in these experiences a boy becomes a man who trusts in the providence of God.

CHAPTER 2

TURNING THE HEARTS AND SECURING THE BONDS

"He will restore the hearts of the fathers to their children and the hearts of the children to their fathers, so that I will not come and smite the land with a curse."
Malachi 4:6

The above verse bringing the Old Testament to an end was especially relevant at the time. Written more than four hundred years before the birth of Jesus, the prophet Malachi spoke to a people who continued to dishonor and drift away from their unique covenant as established with God through their father Abraham. Nevertheless, the words of Malachi 4:6 have never been more pertinent to or needed by any people, culture, or nation than by our own as we negotiate the tumultuous cultural haze and spiritual void of postmodernism in the second decade of the twenty-first century.

Postmodernism as a philosophical doctrine of the academy was stillborn. The evident deficiencies of a system that with belligerence denies any certainty even to revealed truth, necessarily died at its own hand. But what perished quickly in university philosophy classrooms escaped the careful scrutiny of professors and ran wild into the streets contaminating the culture at every point. Now its influence is prevalent in music, in dress, and in the use of drugs and alcohol. A blurring of the distinction between right and wrong and between the barely acceptable and the great are observably almost omnipresent.

Of the many societal and personal casualties resulting from the willful submergence of the modern masses into the philosophical and spiritual cesspool of postmodernism and the coinciding inability or unwillingness of many professed Christians to extricate and wholly separate themselves from it, the separation between a father and his children is arguably the most tragic and consequential. That Malachi spoke of restoring the hearts of the fathers to their children reveals the fact that an active and unbreakable bond between a father and his children was the design and will of God from the beginning. Whether in good times or through days of hardship and struggle, a father's heart is to remain with his children, always moving to and never straying from actions of love and counsel.

Signs of Dad's Absence

Though statistics aplenty abound, revealing the consequences and cost—both to individuals and society—of the absence of a father in the lives of children and young adults, none should need them for the ends of verification. Simply read the daily headlines or go out into the streets and observe with eyes, ears, and mind open. For every young man involved in crime, narcotics, bullying, unprovoked and unjustified violence, or the mistreatment of women (which takes many forms), you will most often find a father by biological definition but a man whose heart is far removed from his son. For every boy without direction, motivation, the desire and drive to achieve, a determination to build his body and strength, and a vision of what can be accomplished in the future, the absence of a father will be easily revealed. For almost every woman who carries the emotional baggage of physical use and abuse, flawed and detrimental relationships with men, drug or alcohol abuse, or who possesses none of the understanding of men and boys requisite for successful and profitable relationships, a father whose heart is distant and whose actions of love are virtually nonexistent is readily observant. Likewise, every girl who will surrender her body and soul to the multifaceted and diabolically driven industries of pornography or prostitution will frequently prove to be the product of a distant and disengaged father.

On either end of the relationships between fathers and children, of course, exceptions can be found. The few—and in this case very few—exceptions, however, as in all matters, only further establish and prove what is the rule. Some will be quick to note individuals matching some of the aforementioned descriptions whom they know to have grown up in "good families" with a father in the home. While having a father present in the home is a good and requisite first step toward success, what must be understood is that the mere physical presence of a father, in and of itself, ensures nothing. A man can sleep every night in the same house with his children yet still give them little or none of his time. His physical proximity to children does not guarantee that his heart is close to them. Being regularly seen and heard in no way equates to the deliberate giving of time, effort, and energy to children on a consistent basis. The body can be present even while the mind, heart, and, most important, the actions of love are very far away.

Power of Dad's Presence

When a father's heart is unrelentingly committed to his children, the greatest manifestation of such commitment is revealed in the amount of quality time that he spends with them. In time spent together between father and son or between father and daughter, love is given action. The action of love and shared experience opens the doors to communication and trust. The sustaining of shared experience keeps those doors open even through disagreement or trying times. Bonds established and secured through shared experience open the hearts and minds of children and young adults to the teaching, counsel, and lessons inherently necessary as they navigate through the challenges, changes, and seasons of life lived.

Different forms of interaction will be needed dependent upon the inclinations and struggles unique to each individual child. However, for those inclined toward the outdoors, wild critters, firearms, and archery—or those who might be so inclined if given an opportunity—there is no shared experience like the hunt to draw the hearts of fathers and their children inextricably and eternally close in a bond that is secure, unbreakable, and impervious to all tests of trials and time. While this effect is markedly profound in the nature of the bond created between fathers and sons, for girls and young women possessed of a passion for the outdoors and the spirit of the hunt, the opportunity for fathers to establish the unique and everlasting bond with their daughters holds the same.

The reasons for the strength and immortality of the bond created through the shared experience of the hunt are many and diverse. One among the reasons, within the span of a mere few decades, has become unique to our time. Simply put, hunting is real.

Virtual Entertainment versus Vivid Reality

Sadly, the only things that many boys and young men—and even men well into their thirties or forties—have shot are zombies or "enemies" on a video game. Never in so many lives has so much time been utterly given and devoted to pursuits of pure fantasy demonstrative of a

Turning the Hearts and Securing the Bonds

contentment to live frivolously in a world of make-believe. The same must be noted for most of what is watched in the countless wasted hours spent in front of television and movie screens. That many—children and adults alike—derive their conceptions of reality and truth from the poppycock and refuse fed to their listless eyes and minds through these media is as obvious as it is pathetic. The costs of such intellectual, spiritual and physical dereliction, both to society and to individuals, are sufficiently extensive and deep as not to be examined in full here but demand the attention of a separate work.

Suffice it to note that carrying, shouldering, and firing a real rifle is nothing like doing the same with a joystick and video game controls. Neither games nor films can impart physical force, physical feeling, or the sense of smell. Even in the visual realm, neither can convey the full magnitude of the splendor and awe of the world's magnificent landscapes or of nature's most powerful forces. Regardless of how supposedly "realistic and gritty" any film or television show is purported to be, they come nowhere near to being able to reveal the sudden surge of adrenaline, excitement, fear, and feelings of smallness and vulnerability that rise palpably and race through every facet of one's being when an elephant, buffalo, rhino or lion springs forward in a full charge. Nor can such duplicate the adrenaline rush and sometimes almost uncontrollable jolt of excitement felt simultaneously by father and son when, after hours of slow stalking, a 10-point buck steps into the clear—the sun gleaming upon massive antlers—for what both know will be but fleeting seconds. The exhilaration that quite remarkably is often felt and demonstrated after scoring a video game "kill" pales to frivolous nothingness in comparison to what is felt at the recoil of a Remington and the subsequent, unmistakable thump of a bullet hitting home on a well-placed shot.

The fantasies of technology and the drama pretended by actors cannot make you feel the bone-chilling cold or the welcome warmth of a wood fire as dusk falls. Through electronic media you cannot smell the first descent of coming snow in the low clouds even before the ground begins to be dusted in white, the pungent scent of the pines on the mountain breeze, or the subtler fragrances of juniper and cedar in the lower country. You do not feel the effects of cold rain or snow upon your body and your steps.

When a game or film ends, there are no tangible or spiritual gains to be taken away. There are no meaningful memories to carry or genuine bonds to be strengthened. At the hunt's end, if the hunters have been blessed to find game and have shot straight, then there is life-sustaining sustenance to be taken home and eaten in the months to come. Regardless of the level of the hunt's success, there are memories of the shared experience to be carried and cherished for a lifetime, hearts drawn closer together and bonds secured, all of which will fortify the individual in the challenges certain to come to every life.

The Gains of Good Company

Aside from the mere reality of the hunt, other aspects inherent in hunting serve to create and strengthen bonds between fathers and children, between men, and sometimes, for men blessed with wives who like to get out and shoot, between husbands and wives. To achieve utmost success, most forms of hunting require that people work together toward the common goal. Two is the absolute minimum, as simply for the sake of safety amid the many potential hazards and dangers of the hunt; none should hunt alone. Besides, the joys of any hunt are greatly enhanced by good company.

The late hunter and author Peter Hathaway Capstick once expressed his passion for the pursuit of game in wild country, for shooting, and for the pleasures of the campfire prepared each night, but he made equally clear that he had no desire to enjoy any of it alone. Contrary to

Turning the Hearts and Securing the Bonds

what many may believe and to the stereotypes of hunters and hunting as often portrayed by media and anti-hunting activists, the harvesting of an animal is but one facet of many in all that is to be enjoyed, achieved, and gained in the hunt. In our view, as will be seen, the taking of game is not even the most important of the objectives and rewards. Companionship and the creation and strengthening of lifelong bonds of family and friendship are far more significant than trophies taken or meat procured. In fact, companionship is just as much treasured and remembered as the capturing of game.

Coming down a shallow river in Alaska, a long-time friend, Pastor Dean Nichols of Kenai, Alaska, decided to help our bear guide by kneeling over the bow of the boat to look for sandbars. We had only about 15 yards of width across the water, and we could hear the big Brownies we were hunting on both sides. Two steps and they would have been unwelcome passengers in our boat. A black bear will maul you but seldom kills. Browns are driven only by the impulse to make it possible for you to meet your Maker face to face. Since it was as dark as midnight in a cypress swamp, the situation was extremely tense.

The devil must have temporarily co-opted my mind. Looking at Dean's expansive posterior and slighted parted legs induced in me an irresistible urge. At this point I was the only one of four in the boat who was armed. I was carrying my .500 Nitro Express double rifle. Taking the barrel I goosed the good pastor right between his legs. He thought a Brownie had him. I never watched a rocket leave the pad so instantly and authoritatively. Temporarily, Dean was out of the boat and ahead of the prow. What saved him from a cold bath in the glacier melt was the apex of his launch, which propelled him to a height that I can only compare to what a pole-vaulter might have attempted. The relatively fast-moving boat was thus able to push forward quickly enough to provide a landing platform for the rapidly descending pastor. When he hit, the thud was so loud that he probably frightened all the bears away—a good thing since all of us were collapsed in uproarious laughter. This was especially the case as the pastor reverted to his pre-conversion argot when he addressed me after his safe, but hard, landing.

A thousand times we have relived this moment. We have laughed ourselves out of many sorrows. The companionship of friends cements the friendship that has no end.

Challenges and Excitement of the Hunt

The challenges of hunting generally come from the animals themselves, the terrain, and the weather, all of which will vary in accordance with the animals and area being hunted. In some parts of Africa, additional challenges can come from unanticipated encounters with wild critters that you are not hunting and whose path you may have no desire to cross. Black mambas, cobras, crocodiles, quick-tempered hippos, cow elephants with young close by, as well as lions and hyenas prowling at the camp's edges in the black of night are among such unsought encounters with which we have had to deal. Challenges on the Dark Continent may also come in the form of surprisingly well-armed bands of roving poachers or in better-armed units of guerilla insurgents. In both scenarios, all choosing not to flee an encounter are generally possessed of a marked inclination to shoot first and ask questions later.

Human Resources

My wife in her love for me is proof that opposites attract. Her idea of "roughing it" is a few nights in a Four Season's Resort with a British High Tea or two included in the package. So we have learned to be aficionados of high tea. In return, she does the adventures with us. We spent a few nights some years ago in Zimbabwe camping by an animal trail down to the Zambezi River. What a lark! All night long a Ringling Brothers parade of animals came by. Crocs, buffalo, rhino,

Turning the Hearts and Securing the Bonds

lions, elephants (everything else scrambled when these behemoths approached) made the journey to water.

About two o'clock in the morning I heard a gentle rustling just outside the tent. Gingerly I opened my window flap, revealing a beautiful 500-pound-plus, black-maned lion only a few feet from the tent. Gently I shook my wife and pointed to the open flap. She looked and said nothing until his majesty passed on to the water. We were in a camp, but it had an African shower and outhouse—in short, all that a woman could want. "If I have to go to the facility, you are going with me," she breathlessly panted. I thought she meant for her protection, so I preened my masculine peacock feathers. She caught the look and interpreted correctly. Then she added, "As bait, buddy!"

Two or More

Wherever and whatever you may be hunting, then, companionship is preferable and usually is necessary. In the rugged canyon country of the Trans-Pecos region of the wilds of western Texas, we often sent one man down to walk the thick brush in the bottom of the canyon. He would not be able to see much but was most likely to flush out deer. A second man walked roughly parallel to him halfway up the slope while a third moved and watched higher up on the rim, allowing for the best possibility of one of the three being able to see and get off a shot at any deer running out. Too, when hunting afoot, there are occasions in which you must make a lengthy run or a quick sprint to get into position for a shot before the animal, through distance or cover, is gone for good. In such situations, the steadying back or shoulder of a companion to still your rifle can be the difference between a shot made or missed.

If a deer was taken in a canyon bottom or down on the slope, then more than one person was usually needed to carry it out. Depending upon whether it was a whitetail or mule deer, the animal could weigh from 80 to over 200 pounds—and in some regions the same can weigh quite a bit more. To carry such weight, in addition to a rifle, water, and any additional supplies, for any distance over uneven ground or through hills, mountains, or canyons, at least two men are needed. Three or four are better still, as two can carry the deer while others carry rifles and supplies.

Field dressing, too, is more quickly and easily accomplished by two than by one. Likewise, to hang a 200-pound deer or an 800-pound elk for skinning is most readily accomplished by at least two men. As we harvest virtually the whole of any deer or elk we take—including neck meat, ribs, and usually the heart and liver—the cutting and packing of the meat with which God has blessed us absolutely necessitates a group effort. Some cut while others wrap and label the packs. Along with her game spirit, wit, and love for the outdoors, my wife Rachel has made herself indispensable to the hunt by becoming a fast and efficient meat packer. As the butchering process is tedious and long work, we usually put on some George Strait, Willie Nelson, Vicente Fernández or Ana Gabriel and break out food and drink to make it as fun as possible. As conversation about anything and everything under the sun surely follows, the more good people the better.

To work with each other and depend upon one another to get food from the field to the table or to take a long sought, magnificent trophy builds and enhances bonds of love, fondness, and devotion as few other shared activities can. While any wholesome shared experiences among friends, family, or father and children are good, none can match the challenge and excitement of the hunt. Thus none can create the same kind of bond.

Mysteries of the Hunt

None, too, except for certain kinds of fishing, can match the mystery of the hunt. You know what game you are after, yet you do not know

Turning the Hearts and Securing the Bonds

when, where, or if you will find it. Will you take a good buck or will it be the one time when "old Mossback," that monster buck often spoken of but seldom seen, stops and looks back in the clear but for a couple of seconds? Will you be able to make the quick shot at 400 yards? Will you have to hit him on the run? Then, exactly how far away is he? How much must you lead him? And how many inches is your .30-06 round going to drop before it gets there? Will you find the deer or elk where you most expect; or will the animal, as often happens, show up when and where you least expect? While occupied with pursuing deer, will a flock of wild turkeys pop up? If so, can you make the shot from 50 to 75 yards with your deer rifle into the base of the neck so that none of the meat is ruined and there are fried wild turkey strips and gravy on the table for Thanksgiving? In parts of Africa where there are scores of game animals to be taken, of course, the mystery only deepens. To delve into the mystery together, to work through it, and then to see it to the end side-by-side entrenches in the mind memories everlasting and intertwines hearts forever—linked in the unspoken but eternal covenant of the hunt.

Number One

We were not even hunting eland on the day I took this high-ranking Livingstone's eland. In fact we saw his tracks—beyond belief! Running with a herd of about 25 in Zimbabwe, we occasionally caught sight of the herd's rear guard; but after six hours of chase, we had never glimpsed the big boy himself. I felt selfish since other hunters were awaiting our return at the Land Rover. I called off the pursuit, noting that he had obviously heard shots before and had little intention of doing so again. Returning to the truck, I pulled my old frame up and looked forward only to be surprised that the herd had circled around and come back to cross the road. And there he was, a magnificent, stately Livingstone's eland—2,200 pounds of surging antelope running on the inside track of the fleeing animals.

Now in my estimation, the best all-purpose rifle for Africa is a .375—a fast bullet with enough knockdown power to take buffalo or even elephant. How I wished for one! What I actually had was a .300 Winchester Magnum; so this had to be a good shot. The elands were at full run, approximately 300 yards away. "Nobody moves!" I shouted, not wishing to have the truck bed shaking. Into the clearing he emerged, and I squeezed the trigger. He never slowed at all. The P.H. (Professional Hunter) said he thought I shot over him. But those remarkable trackers said, "You were right on," and they were off and running. I disembarked from the truck and had walked about 50 yards when I heard the trackers running my way and shouting. Assuming that I had only wounded the eland and he was now the aggressor, I chambered another round and dropped to one knee. The trackers emerged from the bush with big smiles and raised forefingers. "You got number one—the biggest ever!" they shouted.

They were overly optimistic even though he was the biggest they had ever seen. He did go amazingly high in the African Record Book. As I stood looking at that astonishing animal, I was especially thankful for trackers and other companions, including other patient hunters waiting in the truck. We all had a big part in a great eland hunt even though I got to fire the shot.

Vital Gains of Investment

Entailed within the various facets of working together and depending upon one another is the attribute of sacrifice. Fathers and mothers often make financial sacrifices to enable children to hunt. Other adults may do the same for children who are not their own. Many good fathers forego their own pleasures and opportunities in the hunt in order to give a son or daughter the greatest opportunity to take the game being pursued.

Turning the Hearts and Securing the Bonds

My father, along with other men who proved to be vital as mentors and counselors in my own life, did precisely that for me many times over as a boy and young man. By their instruction and counsel, and then by their willingness to stand aside and let me fire misses and make mistakes in situations in which they could easily have taken a deer for themselves, they demonstrated their willingness to make sacrifices on my behalf. Though it took several years for me fully to comprehend and appreciate what they had done, I did eventually understand and never have forgotten. Nor will I ever forget. They believed that the development and maturation of a cocky youth was more important than their own pleasures and gratification, and they acted upon that belief.

Aside from having earned my eternal honor and gratitude to them—honor and gratitude held stronger with each passing year—they kicked down the door to my heart and mind. Because of the lessons they taught about animals, the land, and shooting, because of the fun and unforgettable times they gave to me, the skills and toughness they instilled in me, and because of the sanctuary they afforded me so far from the crowded and noisy confines of the big city that I hated, they ensured that the door, which they had kicked free of its hinges, would never be rebuilt. Those men who had taught me, granted me opportunity, and given me sanctuary could talk to me and be heard, in no uncertain terms, with regard to any subject or aspect of my behavior from that time forward. No other men could approach or admonish me in such a way with any guarantee that I would give ear to or heed their words—not even a pastor, church leader, coach, or teacher.

Far beyond the obvious fact that they had given me many good times and memories, the reason for the splintered door that lay on the ground between me and them and allowed them all access was something much deeper. There was a visceral, innate understanding that they had given me something special and priceless. They had helped me to acquire something that, in my own mind and spirit, was a requisite component of manhood. Even from my earliest years on the hunt, I felt and thought that every man should have the knowledge and the skills to put food on the table straight off the hoof from the bounty of the desert, mountains, plateau, or prairie. While I believed that such capacities should lie within every man, I also knew well that they, in reality, do not. Thus I realized the uniqueness in my own time and place of what these mentors had given to me.

Not many years passed before I knew that so long as I had a firearm or crossbow—and even with bow and arrow I had a fair chance—there was no place in the world upon which animals roamed or fish swam that I could not put food on the table. Not only could I find and harvest the game, but I could process the meat, preserve it, and, with only salt and pepper or with a cabinet full of the spices of the world, could turn the meat into a variety of tasty meals. What came from the ongoing process of learning and the acquisition and sharpening of skills under the eyes and counsel of my father, other men, and one woman was a constant, inviolable, and invaluable line of communication through the invisible door that they had forever opened. Other people, regardless of age or qualifications, I could shut out of my life or ignore, but Dad, Jerry, Freida Kay, Leo, Papa, Larry, and Joe had a lifetime carte blanche to address me with authority on any subject under the sun. To them, even long before I had formulated the depth and implications of it all in my own mind, I had no choice but to listen and to consider with all seriousness their counsel.

Because they had given me knowledge, skills, strength and an edge that I could not have acquired in any other way and, through the process, had given to me and shared with me some of the best and most fun times of my life, I then had no choice but to hear them out whether I agreed with them on a given matter or not. The nature of this access and authority that they held in my life was not one that I would contemplate or fully understand before many years had passed. Rather, it just simply was and could in no way be altered or reversed. As a result, through the long days of hunting in the wild, silent places, at the breakfast table in the dark hours of early morning, at the dinner table at the day's end, and around the fire in the evening the ongoing dialogue between us covered every subject imaginable.

The Rules of Engagement

The conversation could be heated and argumentative, contemplative and calm or downright hilarious, but always the conversation, questions, and counsel went on, not only through the days of the hunt but also to be then carried on at intervals throughout the year. Within the conversation there were only two rules, both of which were unspoken as they were understood by all from the start. There was to be no cursing, and no subject or question was off limits. There was one facet to the conversations that might best be described as simply a reality among us rather than a rule.

A Tumble

It should be noted that this all began before the full emergence of political correctness and that our family neither respects nor abides by political correctness even today. The reality was that anyone who made a stupid mistake either in word or in action could expect to live with it and hear about it for many years to come. If caught using clearly and demonstrably flawed logic in an argument, then you were likely to hear about it again. If your rifle clicked on an empty chamber as a 10-point buck stood broadside 100 yards away, only then to disappear into cover at the sounds of your quickly sliding bolt, then you surely would hear about it again. If you blew a hole through the ceiling or wall of the house with a 30.06 or a .44, then the memory was not likely to die quickly. That at least a couple of holes remain from discharges made more than twenty years ago is sufficiently revealing.

"Watch those loose rocks on the side of the mountain," continued rancher and friend, Jerry Davenport. "I will be careful. I am not that old yet," I assured the group.

"Dad, are you sure you should take the rim?" queried my smart-mouthed 16-year-old son, Armour. "I can handle it," I tersely replied.

The climb was long, and I was a bit winded on arrival but immediately began my regimen. A little ahead of the rest of the group, I found those loose rocks. As footing gave way and I began my long slide to the bottom of the mountain, I knew that it sounded like deer running. Shouts below confirmed this judgment as I heard antiphonal calls of "Deer! Get ready to shoot!"

Now you may suppose that a tumbling 220-pound man would have major concerns with rocks and cactus. Enlightened self-interest, however, made it possible for me to elude some cactus while simultaneously shouting, "Don't shoot!" No use. They could not have hit anything anyway. The whole crew was doubled over at the sight of the overly confident hunter now cascading down the mountainside in a shower of pebbles. Eventually I came to rest at their feet. There is one piece of good news—two of bad. On the happy side, all bones were miraculously intact. On the down side, my body had become the new resident of about six different kinds of cactus, including that woeful dog cactus that you cannot see until you are in it. Not only that, I looked like General Custer after the last moments of the Little Big Horn. To make matters worse, little "ministry" took place then or until now since loud guffaws marred any more eleemosynary actions.

Through it all, in all seasons, and amid challenges and struggles the same as in the good times, the conversations continued. The lessons and counsel that were to form my constitution as a man and change the course of my life forever for the better continued to come through the open door. Although there were other godly adults to whom I would

Turning the Hearts and Securing the Bonds

listen with regard to certain subjects and situations, only those noted herein held exclusive and lifelong access to come through the doorway and to speak upon any and all matters. Such access they gained and held because of our shared experience in a primal, masculine endeavor rooted in the spirit of almost every red-blooded boy and man. To paraphrase the prophet Malachi, by turning their hearts to me through a medium that resonated in my spirit and soul, they turned my heart, fully open unto them (Malachi 4:6).

CHAPTER 3

THE GLORY OF YOUNG MEN

*The glory of young men is their strength,
And the honor of old men is their gray hair.*
Proverbs 20:29

The glory of young men is their meek spirit, orderly behavior, politeness, the eagerness to lift voice in sweet songs of worship, and effort to participate in harmonious ringing of handbells to the melodies of hymns, or so I was led to believe by most in positions of authority while growing up in the church. Such a soft, safe, delicate, and feminized utopia may seem wonderful, and it may feel spiritually and emotionally uplifting to many. The problem is that such an agenda for boys and young men is contrary to, and the polar opposite of, the ideal as stated in Scripture.

None of these activities is inherently wrong. In fact, meekness is among the noblest virtues of strength. Although none could ride Alexander's horse, the conqueror's steed was called "a meek horse" because he was fully controlled by the general. Properly defined, all of these other activities exhibit strength. But in isolation or without the accompaniment of decidedly masculine activities, a young man will not follow.

Mysteries of the Bush

Proverbs 20:29 reveals clearly and absolutely that the glory of young men is their strength. No alternative options of measure or pursuit for the glory of young men are offered. Nor is any praise or credit of young men to be found in the pages of the Bible that does not involve the manifestation of strength in at least one of its various forms. Having such an indisputably clear statement from Scripture, I long have marveled and wondered why churches generally do not teach and strongly encourage all of their healthy young men to pursue the building of strength. In the face of this degree of clarity, any excuse for not so doing becomes difficult to justify.

Most activities within the church for boys and young men are not designed to encourage the building of strength. Furthermore, they offer precious little by which the foundations of genuine learning and of wisdom, knowledge, discernment, and understanding can begin to be established. Serious though these shortcomings are in and of themselves, they do not constitute the worst of the consequences.

In my own childhood, despite undoubtedly having honorable intentions, those who wanted to teach me to sing, ring bells, perform skits, dress me in a pretty choir robe, or fit me properly in a feminine costume were actually driving me away from everything that had anything to do with church. Their effect upon the hearts and minds of many other young males was the same. You can also be certain that most of the older men who decided to visit to see what the church was about, upon seeing such displays, found little to impress or endear them. Pressing boys and young men essentially to behave like girls and young women is lacking in logic, wisdom, and in any scriptural mandate.

Boys and young men have sufficient natural inclinations toward certain levels of rebellion without the adults in authority over them intensifying the problem by actually giving them a valid reason for it. Purveyors of politeness, panty hose, meekness, skits, song, and handbells had no inlet either to my heart and mind or to those of most other boys and young men. Once given a valid reason for rebellion—one I felt was substantiated by the essence and attributes of manhood as revealed in the honorable and faithful men of the Bible—they had not the platform, medium, or opening with which to reach me. Only those who taught me to ride, stalk, shoot, cut, and to live off the land held such access. Fortunately, all were godly and were devoted to training up boys and young men to become strong, self-sufficient, and loving men of God in the molds of the great men of the Bible.

THE WAYS TO A BOY'S HEART

To be sure, there are other masculine endeavors by which fathers and mentors, through shared experience, might gain access to the minds and hearts of sons and young men. Learning to build things, to repair or rebuild vehicles, travel or hike in remote places, participate in equine sports and rodeo, or engage in athletic pursuits or martial arts are a few examples of wholesome, productive activities by which strength and skills can be built, lessons taught, and access gained. My father and I regularly boxed, wrestled, traveled together on trips short and far away, and competed in basketball, tennis, racquetball, ping pong, bowling, and pool. Too, we shared many a greasy spoon delicacy—just he and I—from charcoal-broiled burgers and fries to plates of Texas barbecue and tall stacks of manhole-sized pancakes. Never underestimate the power of tasty food that sticks to the ribs in a down-home atmosphere to open doors to boys and young men. With that being acknowledged, it should be understood that there is no shared endeavor that can develop strength in tandem with a unique set of invaluable and steadily fading skills and knowledge to the degree as can be accomplished in the hunt. Too, for many boys and young men, none other can facilitate so strong a bond or so complete an opening of heart.

Strength

To understand what is asserted here, you must first apprehend the nature of strength—the glory of young men. Strength has multiple facets. There is the raw power, for example, needed to lift and carry a deer out of a canyon. There is the strength measured by endurance, such as in walking as much as 10 or 12 miles in a day on rocky ground (far different than walking on a treadmill or track) in hills or mountains while carrying the weight of rifle and pack, sitting in the saddle while remaining continually alert for ten hours, or carrying a harvested animal for a long distance over difficult terrain. Then there is the strength of perseverance of body and mind through extremes of weather and temperature.

Mind over Matter

As dawn broke on the final morning of my last elk hunt in the White Mountains of Arizona, I was standing in two feet of snow and a steady wind with a temperature of 3° F. I have hunted on bitter days when the snow came more horizontally than falling down. One brutal winter day in west Texas when far from house or vehicle, my hands once became so cold as to lose full mobility. To reload my rifle, normally accomplished with just the thumb and forefinger of one hand as a round is pressed down into the magazine, I actually had to rest the rifle in my lap and use two hands to get the cartridge properly inserted. Some of the most miserable days came when the temperature stayed a bit above freezing as the rain continually fell.

Mental toughness—the fortitude and determination of the mind to keep pressing on relentlessly toward an objective even in the midst of adverse weather, bad luck, injury, or any other obstacle—is another form of strength developed when boys and young men hunt. Hunting in many regions is far more challenging than most who do not hunt may realize. Wild animals seldom show up when and where you want them to. They often are not where they "should be." This is due to a reality soon learned by all who hunt in wild country. There is only one hard, fast, and absolutely certain rule with regard to the behavior of wild critters: There are no hard, fast, and absolutely certain rules. There are patterns and tendencies, some of which may hold ninety-nine percent of the time, but there are no sureties. Young men who hunt learn that just as in life, there are no guarantees, and you usually will not get what you are pursuing unless you are willing to weather storms, fight adversity, and deal with setbacks, all the while keeping the mind focused upon the objective and task at hand.

Skill-at-Arms

Strength, too, has been measured by a man's skills and formidability with weaponry from the beginning, from the earliest formations of tribes and states, and through all of history. Nowhere are men of valor and skill-at-arms any more honored and commended than in Scripture. Dismiss any rubbish you may have heard suggesting that once you have Jesus, you no longer need be concerned with weapons. Jesus, before He gave Himself up to go to the cross, in one of His last commands to the men who followed Him and would carry out His message to the world, commanded them that if they had no sword they were to sell their coats and buy one. No other rational interpretation exists for this command in Luke 22:36 except that Jesus would rather that they suffer from cold—and winter in much of the Bible lands is quite cold—than to be unarmed. Understand that the swords of which Jesus spoke were not showpieces or collectibles, as is evidenced by the effect of Peter's blade on Malchus in John 18:10. In the hands of strong men who knew how to use them, they were life-takers and heartbreakers.

David did not sing and play his harp into power, though his melodious voice and skill on the harp were legendary. He fought his way to power, supplementing his martial skills with savvy diplomacy when necessary. Abraham, as recounted in Genesis 14, did not take back his people and property from the marauding four kings from the east with fiery rhetoric. He did so on a nocturnal raid with bloodied swords. Once the walls of Jericho fell at the shouts of the men, Joshua did not conquer with a choir and handbells. He conquered leading men with swords, spears, and shields. Ehud did not free Israel from the yoke of Moab by giving the fat Moabite king Eglon extra doughnuts. He freed Israel by surreptitiously burying an eighteen-inch blade in Eglon's bulging stomach (Judges 3:15-25). David did not pay the dowry for Saul's daughter Michal with Sunday School cookies or extra sets on the harp. He doubled the dowry of a hundred Philistine foreskins with two hundred foreskins. Do understand that Philistine soldiers neither offered these freely nor gave them up easily. Gideon did not stop the fast-moving raids of the Midianites with pleas for kindness. He defeated them with superior strategy and tactics in a night-time attack, scattering them and putting many, including their leaders, Oreb and Zeeb, to the sword (Judges 7). The mighty men of valor honored and praised numerous times through the books of Samuel, Kings, and Chronicles did not earn their distinction and honor through uplifting skits. They earned such solely through courageous and skillful deeds with weaponry on the battlefield. Benaiah did not kill the lion in a pit on a snowy day with harsh reprimands (2 Samuel 23:20). He likely did so with a spear.

Why would Benaiah jump down into a pit in the snow with an African lion when the beast, one of the most formidable killers on earth, could have been more easily, not to mention much more safely, killed from on top? Many may not understand this, but most red-blooded hunting men will. Benaiah did it because he was a strong man and because he could. Perhaps he was a true sporting man as well, wanting to be sure that such a magnificent creature had a fair chance. Too, there was nothing to brag about, and no glory to be had, if the lion was killed from complete safety. Benaiah did not merely want to kill something.

What he wanted was the challenge, the danger, and the struggle—the struggle against the elements and against one of the most powerful and proficient killers in the animal kingdom. For this reason he deliberately put himself into a situation in which there could be no retreat and no change of mind. Either man or beast or both would be killed.

If hunters only wanted to kill things, as many who oppose hunting commonly and erroneously assert, then they would all be working for Tyson, Oscar Meyer, and the like in slaughterhouses. What hunters desire is the challenge and the bounty of the hunt. They want to test themselves against the terrain, the elements, and the wit, power, speed, and often-superior senses of the game. They want to hone their skills with rifle, pistol, bow, and spear. And yes, I do know men who hunt and have taken game with spears and with large knives. In the end, they want to enjoy the delicious and wholesome protein, often amid retellings of the memories of how it was taken.

Thirst for the Thrill

Often I am asked, "What was your favorite hunt?" My reply is, "The next one." But I know what is being asked. And the answer for which the interrogator is fishing lies somewhere among the lion, cape buffalo, leopard, elephant, hippo, and brown bear—all fraught with danger and a charge from the animal—these I relive a thousand times. We have made a few "sensational" shots, and these are okay, but nothing compared with a charging buffalo.

In fact, some of the most memorable encounters occurred with no shot even fired. Pursuing a large bull elephant in a herd of about thirty in Zimbabwe one day provided two memorable encounters. The first happened quite unexpectedly. In close single file and walking through the dense bush as quietly as possible, the tracker turned and whispered to me, "We are close. Be ready." Thirty more steps and there across the five-inch trail was an elephant tail. The tracker, looking ahead, failed to see it until his right foot was descending. His discovery provided no time to reflect, so he erroneously concluded that the tail was a black mamba. I still do not know how he reversed himself from that step commitment, but I do know that he hit me coming back. I hit the man behind me, and so forth to the end of the line of six. We looked like dominoes falling. The commotion awakened the sleeping giant, who, incredibly, had deposited himself on a carpet of green and was peacefully snoozing unaware of approaching trouble.

Bleary-eyed from the rude interruption, the elephant gazed over his pursuers from his towering position as they floundered about on the floor of the bush. The decision of this 15-year-old was whether to charge or flee. Righting ourselves, four rifles were focused between his eyes. Though enormous already, he still had about ten years to grow, so we did not want to shoot the young bull. Suddenly, he turned and with the sound of a tsunami exited our presence. Then we all breathed. While it seemed like a six-hour ordeal, the whole event was over in less than two minutes. Being five feet away from a sleep-deprived, young bull elephant threatening charge can never be forgotten.

After a suitable pause to recover our legs and stomachs, we continued on and in thirty minutes found the herd. Several females had calves. Not good news. The big bull stayed conveniently out of the range of my 500. We kept pressing in, and the bull would send the angered females to protect their calves. Suddenly, the P.H. offered a startled observation: "How in the ____ did that happen?" We were completely surrounded by females that were short on patience about the intrusion. "If we have to run, do not run in a straight line, and throw your clothes off as you run," continued the professional hunter. "Do you really think that at age sixty-three I am going to outrun that elephant?" I asked as the bulky madam closed to within 40 feet. "Besides, if I threw off my clothes, there would be a *Baptist Press* photographer in every tree," I confidently observed.

The Glory of Young Men

"Are you running?" asked my son-in-law, Mark Howell. "Of course not," came the reply of the professional hunter. "Then this is a standoff," I shouted, adding a threat to my son-in-law. "If you ever tell my daughter what I got you into, God being my helper, you are a dead preacher," I whispered. I still could not tell you how we got out. No shot was fired, but it was among the most unforgettable thirty minutes of all of our lives.

Not only do red-blooded boys and young men desire and even crave such challenges. They need to have those challenges put before them both to feed their spirits and to develop strength of mind, body, spirit, and resolve. They need to develop the strength of the knowledge of, and skill at, arms. The greater the training in weaponry, the better. They need to learn how to feed themselves and their dependents in any time, place, and situation, and how to survive outdoors in harsh extremes. Finally, they need to build the self-confidence that comes in the accumulation of it all. Those boys and young men showing no desire or inclination for such challenges, in most cases, are likely in greater need of them than are those who crave the challenge.

Valor

Given the ease of life made possible by affluence and technology, some would question the value, let alone the necessity, of young men building strength and developing the age-old skills of proficiency in weapons and outdoor survival. Yes, millions of them seem to be getting along fine while possessing no such strength or skills. So why, in our soft, insulated modern times, should young men be encouraged to build strength and skills through hunting and other masculine endeavors?

The primary reason is that the world remains, as it always has been, a bad and dangerous place. Anyone able merely to read simple headlines should be reminded of that fact on a daily basis. Furthermore, truth does not change with trends and times, and thus the truth of scriptural precepts and principles remains as penetrating, relevant, and vital as it has been from the beginning. That young men should aspire and work to build strength in all of the aforementioned facets, for Christians, is an unavoidable and unchanging mandate of God Himself.

Aside from the biblical mandate, though, there are practical and logical reasons to guide young men toward the building of strength and skills, the fact that remains the ultimate reason for the scriptural mandate. Young men, in accordance with what must be taken from the totality of Scripture, are meant to be protectors and providers. They protect the nation on the battlefield, at sea, and in the air. In various police agencies, the daily protection of citizens and property in cities and countryside falls upon their shoulders. In cities, mountains, deserts, and on the prairies, they fight the raging fires that threaten property, land, and life. Men provide, or at least should do so, the first line of protection for the women and children in their homes. Young men also must provide the bulk of the rescues and ground relief in times of natural or manmade disaster. We witnessed many examples of this in New York on September 11, 2001; in New Orleans after Katrina; as well as in the numerous natural disasters occurring since, as the injured and stranded were rescued, treated, and carried to safety. In addition to these various forms of the provision of protection, security, and aid, men, at the most basic level, must be providers of food and shelter for their own and for those unable to help themselves in any situation that comes.

While the most important aspect of the preparation of young men for most of the aforementioned tasks is the quality of the training received from the respective agencies, the import of the core of their education, training, and development in the early formative years cannot be ignored or understated. Not all policemen, soldiers, firefighters, or other first responders having received the same training are equal in capability or performance. If they were equal, then promotions would become a difficult proposition, and the accomplishments and deeds of none would stand out and above any others. The fact is, though, that in every job and field, some do stand conspicuously above the majority of their peers in capacities and in deeds accomplished.

Standouts

That the deadliest and most accomplished sniper in United States history, Carlos Hathcock, was a country boy who grew up hunting in rural Arkansas is not coincidence. The diminutive Audie Murphy, who, by his phenomenal exploits in World War II, emerged as the most highly decorated American soldier of the war, grew up hunting, shooting, and fighting frequently in rural northeast Texas. One of the twelve siblings abandoned by their father, he shot squirrels and rabbits just to put food on the table. Even as a young boy, his aim became so deadly that, with an old .22 rifle, he could hit rabbits on the run consistently, and apparently could do so even when shooting out the window of a moving car.

Frank Hamer, the best-known and most accomplished Texas Ranger of the modern era—the man who tracked down Bonnie and Clyde and sent them to the grave after numerous officers in other states had failed—grew up cowboying, hunting, and shooting in the wilds of the trans-Pecos region of western Texas. Though he no longer dressed like a west Texas cowboy, the toughness, savvy, and skills he developed in the rugged Chihuahuan Desert served him well against many of the most evil men in both city and countryside.

Vasily Zaitsev, the best known and one of the most deadly Russian snipers in World War II, grew up hunting deer and wolves with his grandfather in the Ural Mountains. In roughly five weeks in the Battle of Stalingrad, he killed 225 German soldiers, and had killed more than 400 by the war's end. Numerous other Russian snipers with confirmed kills ranging well into the hundreds also came from rural backgrounds in which they honed their rifle skills on the hunt from days of boyhood.

Others—even boys and girls—joined the shooting clubs that became popular in the U.S.S.R. in the 1930s. Lyudmila Mykhailivna Pavlichenko joined one such club in Kiev when she was around fourteen years old. By the war's end, she had made 309 confirmed kills against the Nazis. Between the snipers with extensive hunting experience and the proliferation of shooting clubs, the U.S.S.R., at the onset of World War II, may have been the closest thing to a true nation of riflemen since the days of the American Revolution and the early Republic. The fact proved to be a key factor in holding off and ultimately defeating an army that was better armed, better organized, and technologically superior to their own. The snipers wreaked havoc on the Nazi war machine not only by the number of soldiers they took out of action but also by targeting and taking out field officers and non-commissioned officers whom the Germans found increasingly difficult to replace as the war dragged on. With the constant loss of comrades to an unseen enemy virtually impossible to locate and hit and the sustained loss of officers and resulting breakdowns of order, discipline, and continuity, morale began to plummet.

What becomes clear in retrospect is that the Soviet riflemen—and rifle-women—were a key factor in holding off the superior Nazi war machine through the darkest days of the war. On paper, a Nazi victory appeared certain, but wars are not fought on paper. And no matter the extent to which technology advances, wars are ultimately determined by the leadership and by the shooters on the ground.

"White Death"

Interestingly, prior to Stalingrad and the defense of Moscow, the Soviets were to get what could be considered "a taste of their own medicine" from an unexpected source. In the winter of 1939, Soviet armed forces invaded Finland with the objective of complete conquest. Given the vast inferiority of Finland's manpower and military hardware, it seemed, on paper at least, that complete victory was assured and would come quickly.

Along with a determined Finnish resistance at all levels, however, the soldiers of the Red Army came up against something that they called the "White Death." The "White Death," actually a quiet and simple man, was not even a professional soldier. Before deciding to join his fellow Finns in resistance after the Soviet invasion, Simo Häyhä was known by those in his rural region for only three things. He was a farmer, an avid hunter, and the winner of many trophies in his country's popular shooting contests.

Less than a hundred days after the opening shots, when the Winter War came to an end with the Moscow Peace Treaty in March of 1940, Simo Häyhä, covered in white from head to foot as he moved unseen over the deep snow, had killed well over 700 Soviet soldiers. Five hundred forty-two of those kills were confirmed, making him the deadliest known sniper from any nation, in any war, in history. All of this he accomplished with a simple bolt-action rifle with iron sights, shunning the use of the telescopic sights—used by virtually all snipers then as now—so as to lessen his chances of being spotted. What is more remarkable is that he did so, and survived (living to the age of 96) going up against many good shooters, and likely the world's best snipers of that time, on the other side.

For a simple farmer and hunter to have stepped into war against one of the world's most powerful armies, which also boasted many of the best shooters, and to have accomplished what he did, reveals more than the obvious. His marksmanship and mastery of the rifle are apparent enough, but he also had to have developed all facets of the strength requisite to hard hunting and to have honed the various skills inherent therein. Stamina, endurance of and perseverance through miserable and potentially lethal weather, mental toughness, determination to stay the course, the abilities to move unseen and in silence even when cover is minimal, and the aptitude for stillness and patience all are evident in his lethality and survival. More important to his homeland was the fact that, though Finland lost some territory, she retained her sovereignty. Due in part to the demoralizing effect of the heavy losses inflicted by Häyhä and the shooters like him, the vastly superior Red Army was forced to abandon its objective of complete conquest. Among other lessons, we can learn that a nation of proficient riflemen, regardless of disadvantages in numbers, hardware, or technology, never stands helpless or without a chance before any enemy—be the enemy from the outside or from within.

Defenders and Protectors

Although this work is not a preparation manual for combat or war—and is not intended to be—the tragic truth as penned by George Santayana remains upon the shoulders of the living forever. Only the dead have seen the end of war. The ravages and heartbreak of war are felt by all, but men have always borne the brunt of battle—and the young men in particular, as they are the ones who do the preponderance of the killing and the dying and who bear the foremost physical and psychological scars.

For example, Brian Vickers, a Canadian serving as sergeant-at-arms in the Canadian parliament, had with him his pistol in a strangely liberal Canadian society when an invader entered Parliament on October 22, 2014. His quick thinking and sharp shooting took out a potential killer and saved many lives. One has to wonder why people still do not get the point. A public with good people armed is a safe public.

Young men who lean toward careers in military service or law enforcement will benefit from the varied combination of skills acquired through properly supervised hunting, just as did each of the aforementioned men who distinguished themselves and survived against formidable adversaries in dire conditions. Furthermore, all young men—especially those who will not train for law enforcement or for military service—need to know how to defend their homes in an increasingly violent and dangerous world. They must be able and ready to protect their wives, children, and other dependents in the street, on the road, and in the backcountry. For such ends they are given strength and capacities for aggression and ferocity by their Creator.

Masculine Virtues

Hunting is by no means the only way by which to teach young men the masculine virtues of martial skill, toughness, resilience, endurance, resourcefulness, determination and confidence. In fact, even boys and young men who hunt should be encouraged to engage in other masculine and martial pursuits such as boxing, wrestling, other martial arts, weightlifting, running, fencing, target-shooting, archery, and manually chopping wood. All such activities work in conjunction to build the various facets of strength, which are, according to the Bible, the glory of young men. All build the strength requisite for them to be prepared to fill the roles for which they are created, fortified, and designated. None, however, so aptly combines the glory of young men with the honor of old men as does the properly executed hunt. None can any more fruitfully combine the building of young men's strength with the counsel and wisdom of the older men's graying heads.

A hunt has many more components than are often realized. Among those are the opportunities for fathers, grandfathers, uncles, and mentors to lead and teach life lessons to the young. In the conversations and interaction that flows—as naturally as a mountain stream—in the hours spent gathered around the campfire or hearth, on the long walks or rides, through the long hours of preparing and packaging meat, or gathered around the table for venison steaks, the wisdom marked by years and graying heads is slowly but steadily imparted to the minds and hearts of the young.

The nature of such interaction between the old and the impassioned youth, and the natural ease with which it flows and is received, can be duplicated in few other environments or activities. Unfortunately, for most boys and young men, it constitutes a level of intellectual and spiritual openness that will never be matched in the kinds of activities offered by most churches or by schools, and it surely cannot be equaled by families or groups sitting around while absorbed by the contents of a television screen, computers, or cell phones. The vastness and inherent solitude of the wild places allows for levels of thought and interaction simply not attainable amid the noise, bustle, and frivolous, unceasing activity of the urban and suburban centers. Further, the fact that hunting, and all the preparations and activities that accompany it, stimulate and excite the innate characteristics and inclinations of the masculinity set within boys and young men by their Creator, leaves them more open to any wisdom or counsel coming from the men who make possible the hunt and engage therein with them. Put more simply, most young men and boys will be more willing to listen to any man teaching them to ride, shoot, track, identify game, clean and maintain weapons, and dress and prepare wild game than to a man who wants to teach them to sing, ring bells, give emotional testimonies, or to play sweetly with others.

The men who taught me all of these things, and also how to punch, block, cut, thrust, parry, drive trucks and land rovers in rough country, ride motorcycles, take care of animals, catch fish, drive boats, make camps, and to survive in extremes of climate and terrain kicked open the door to my mind and heart, which, to them, would never again be closed. Because they taught me all of these things and more, which, to many modern minds, may seem lacking in spiritual import or current relevance, they were then able to teach me to love, forgive, pray, care for the needy and the suffering, to pursue righteousness and peace, to give of myself and my resources, to live in gentleness, and always to speak and stand for the truth. Thus virtues and commitments that may seem wholly unrelated to hunting or to the development of masculine skills and engagement of manly inclinations were, in fact, predominantly the very product of such. Only those who taught me and who engaged with me in masculine endeavors had the requisite inroads for them to teach me the far more important lessons of life.

A Common Bond

You can never know when the skills acquired through hunting and other masculine endeavors, which may not be highly praised or encouraged in many churches, will actually open doors in sharing the gospel of Jesus Christ. In our experience, this has happened quite often in foreign countries whose cultures have not been beset by the political correctness and feminization that grips our own modern culture.

A Bridge across Cultures

Once, while on a mission trip in the backcountry of the predominantly Muslim Kazakhstan, a wealthy herdsman on the steppes, who had never before seen an American, was determined to show us his hospitality by slaughtering a lamb and hosting us for dinner. As he prepared to cut the lamb's throat, much to the dismay of a few of the left-leaning members of our American group, he suddenly stopped as he saw the glint off the long, razor-sharp clip-point blade that I had drawn from beneath the concealment of my bloused shirt. He immediately set down his old and much used blade and reached eagerly for mine. After examining the edge with a passing thumb, he flashed a wide, approving smile and then put the knife into action. When the lamb had bled out, he began the process of removing the skin, and as he was working alone, I took my knife, knelt down and began skinning on the opposite leg. He smiled again in a seeming mix of surprise, approval, and gratitude.

True to the ways of his people and culture, he was going to show us his hospitality regardless. Nevertheless, what became quickly evident to all present was that, upon seeing the knife initially and then to observe my ability and willingness to get down on the ground and help him skin the lamb—and to do so properly—produced an instant and palpable change in his demeanor toward us. In two men from countries far apart and cultures and religions profoundly different, there was, in merely the simplest of gestures and acts, suddenly a common thread and bond.

Kazakhstan, like all Muslim strongholds, is a difficult place to which to take the gospel, and I cannot proclaim with certainty anything with regard to the herdsman's eternal soul. What I can say with certainty is that, following these simplest of acts and the revealing of the common threads between us, he was open to us and to the message we brought in a way and to a degree that he would not have been otherwise. On those same steppes, I also rode with and raced horses with other Kazakhs. I wrestled against their strong and skilled young men and generally got the worst of it. The Kazakhs are a strong, spirited, and virile people. Yet the fact that I competed with them and demonstrated a familiarity with certain things appreciated and valued by them—horses, blades, pastoral life, good leather work, and man-on-man, *mano a mano* competition—opened them to our message and example to a degree probably unattainable by any other method. Some came to Christ and in the hearts of others seeds were planted. Much, and in some cases perhaps most, of the human force that opened doors to minds and hearts, came as the result of skills and attitudes acquired in hunting and in certain other masculine endeavors. Suffice it to note that singing to them, preaching polished sermons, or giving impassioned testimonies probably would not have left as much of an impression or opened as many doors as when coupled with immersing ourselves into their world.

A Platform for Life Lessons

Simply to go afield with a son, daughter, or another youth and shoot an animal, and then promptly send off its parts to a taxidermist and meat processor, in and of itself, accomplishes little or nothing. Yet on properly planned and carried-out hunts, in which all facets of hunting—the before, during, and after, so to speak—are seen through, and in which the old and the young engage in all activities that surround and are a part of the hunt together, the stage is then set not only for the acquisition of an increasingly rare skill set but also for the teaching and learning of the greater and most important lessons of life. There, in mountains, desert, forest, bushveld, jungle, or on prairie or savanna, the wisdom and counsel of graying heads can merge with the vigor, strength, and struggles of youth in a way wholly unique, special, and rewarding to all who so engage. Always, therein, what stands in the balance to be yielded down the line in the quests and battles of life is much greater and more significant than the harvest yielded from any hunt.

To this point, we have told nothing about the greatest strengths to be sought and developed by men and boys. Character, responsibility, faithfulness, moral integrity, knowledgeability of the words and ways of God are the greatest achievements that men may master. And these are strengths that a quadriplegic who never had the opportunity to venture into the field can muster, perhaps more profoundly so than the hunter. But please make no mistake. If we care about our social order, if our children are generally to develop these and other forms of prowess, there is little substitute for a dad or granddad in the field or in the stream with his boys. The choice is yours, Dad.

CHAPTER 4

HUNTING AND LIFE

*A lazy man does not roast his prey,
But the precious possession of a man is diligence.*
Proverbs 12:27

For all who follow Jesus Christ and live by the precepts and principles of Judeo-Christian Scripture, hunting is not only a venture of multifarious profit but also is a portion of our biblical heritage. Although seldom considered in this way and even less often so presented, the biblical significance and import of the hunt is indisputable, and we can know its importance by the numerous references and analogies to hunting and to wildlife throughout the Bible.

First, understand that the Levant and most of the Middle East, the region in which most biblical events transpired, held an abundance of wildlife throughout the Old and New Testament periods. Even in recent years, we have seen gazelles, ibex, and leopards in the south of Israel in the precious little wild country that remains there. In biblical times, such animals, along with a variety of other critters surviving now in the wild predominantly in Africa, roamed in far greater numbers across the bulk of the land. Lions, hyenas, Nile crocodiles, hippopotamuses ("Behemoth" described in Job 40:15-24), Arabian oryx, and ostriches are among the African critters common to regions of the lands of the Bible—likely more common than some people in biblical times would have wished. Wolves, roebucks, and Syrian brown bears were among the non-African species prevalent then. In 2 Kings 2:24, two Syrian brown bears avenged the prophet Elisha by severely mauling forty-two of the ill-mannered lads who had mocked Elisha's bald head. These were the same bears, along with lions, about which David spoke of killing before his fight with Goliath in the Elah Valley in 1 Samuel 17:36.

Second, know that when any speaker uses an analogy to make a point, he is attempting to focus upon some activity, event, or behavior to which the vast majority of his audience will relate due to their inherent knowledge and understanding of it. The Bible contains many references and analogies regarding dangerous wildlife and encounters with such. Therein are also to be found numerous analogies in which a point is made through illustrations of the hunt.

The Bible is not a book filled with intriguing accounts of the hunt because these thrilling stories were not part of the purpose for which they were shared and recorded. Holy Scripture was given to reveal truth and to make known the laws and ways of the living God. While the hunting exploits of kings and nobles in biblical times have been attested by historical and archaeological records, we can also know that many other men in those days engaged in the hunt simply by the fact that so many biblical analogies used the well understood concepts of hunting to drive home a point.

Biblical Allusions

In the Bible's earliest reference to hunting in Genesis 10:9, we learn that Nimrod "was a mighty hunter before the Lord." Interestingly, we know little else about him, just that he was formidable and strong—"a mighty one on the earth"—and that he was a strong and skilled hunter.

Hunting and Life

Verses 8 and 9, as little as they reveal of the man, are there for a reason. For all young men to aspire to be strong, formidable men and skilled hunters—and thus good providers and protectors—before the Lord, submitting to Him and to His ways, would be sufficient reason by biblical standards.

In 1 Samuel 26:20, David compares his plight at Saul's paranoid, murder-bent pursuit, to a partridge being hunted in the mountains. In Isaiah 13:14, the prophet compares the condition of the people before the terrifying judgment of the Lord to be like that of "a hunted gazelle." Speaking of the restoration of His people in Jeremiah 16:16, God says through the prophet, "I will send for many hunters, and they will hunt them from every mountain and every hill and from the clefts of the rocks." In the Lamentations of Jeremiah, in verse 52 of chapter 3, the prophet speaks of his enemies hunting him down like a bird. Condemning the false prophets of Israel in Ezekiel 13:20-21, the Lord accuses them of hunting the lives of their people as if they were birds and promises to tear the people from their grasp so that "they will no longer be in your hands to be hunted." In Ezekiel 34, verses 8 and 22, the prophet again drives home his point by declaring that his people had become the "prey" of the hunters due to the neglect and abuse of the religious leaders, the shepherds of Israel. In condemning the injustice and oppression of the wealthy and powerful in Isaiah 59:14-15, Isaiah notes that those who turned away from evil marked themselves as "prey" in the eyes of the wicked who would hunt and strike them down.

Reflecting the people's familiarity with the awesome power, speed, and stealth of the large predatory animals are the analogies utilizing the prowess of the lion and bear. In Job 10:16, the afflicted servant of the Lord says, "Should my head be lifted up, You would hunt me like a lion." In Amos 5:18-19, the bold shepherd-prophet of Tekoa issued an unnerving admonition to those who lived in unrighteousness yet claimed to long for the day of the Lord. For them, he warned, that day would be, "As when a man flees from a lion and a bear meets him, or goes home, leans his hand against the wall and a snake bites him." In Psalm 22:21, David, knowing well the strength and lethality of the predators, prays to be saved "from the lion's mouth." In 1 Peter 5:8, the fiery fisherman-turned-disciple of our Lord compares our adversary Satan to a prowling lion in search of prey. Finally, in the reference to the unmatched power and glory of our Lord Jesus Christ—and in testimony to the prevalence of lions in Judah at the time—Revelation 5:5 announces that the Lion of the tribe of Judah has overcome.

Our biblical heritage of strong, independent men of faith able and willing to provide, protect, and fight for a just cause comes down to us from all of the aforementioned men of valor and skill as well as from many others, some of whom are named in the pages of Scripture and some who are not. Such a heritage cannot be relegated to sentimental remembrance or a mere fact of history long passed. Rather, this heritage constitutes a mandate of our God with regard to the kind of Christian men we are to train up and turn out.

The Legacy of Ishmael

Few would dispute Abraham as our earthly father in the faith, for his stature as such is confirmed in both the Old and New Testaments. Yet the man who first and most concretely set forth and established our heritage as strong and skilled hunters before the Lord, as well as exemplifying the roles of provider, protector, and faithful leader, is usually missed or ignored and often is shunned and vilified. Ishmael came from Abraham's seed and, as Abraham's firstborn son, received through the covenant between his father and the living God a blessing unique, unprecedented, and never again to be granted to any other in all of Scripture or history except his brother Isaac.

God's special covenant for the people chosen and set apart by Him to manifest His light, His ways, His laws, and His most profound blessings unto all peoples of the world was to run solely through Isaac. Concerning this fact there can be neither doubt nor debate. However, God's blessings and purposes in the covenant with Abraham were also to extend to Ishmael and his descendants. The children of Isaac would be *the* uniquely chosen people of God to bring the Messiah and thus redemption for the world. The children of Ishmael, while not directly receiving law and Scripture or having a place in the genealogy from which the Messiah was to descend in Advent, were also a chosen people.

The magnitude of the promise made to Hagar by the angel of the Lord regarding Ishmael and the blessings then bestowed upon him and his descendants was surpassed only by the promises made to Abraham regarding Isaac and the subsequent blessings manifested upon him and his descendants. Upon none other were the blessings granted to Ishmael to find an equivalent. Nor would any other be promised so much.

Only Isaac and Ishmael carried the promise, through the seed of Abraham, to become great nations with descendants too numerous to be counted. No other man or people were so chosen and blessed. Yet while Isaac, the second son of Abraham, is rightfully revered, Ishmael—Abraham's firstborn son—if not ignored completely, is most commonly assigned the role of villain and antagonist to Isaac and to the ways and plan of God. Furthermore, Ishmael's modern descendants are seen and portrayed as natural, and even biblically mandated, antagonists and enemies to all Christians and Jews. The fact is one as unfortunate as it is erroneous.

Common Misunderstandings

While the whole of the place of Ishmael in Scripture and God's divine plan for his descendants as made manifest therein lay beyond the scope of this work, a rudimentary understanding of the man, his blessing, and his time and place will prove useful to our purposes. In lockstep with the common portrayal of Ishmael as antagonist or villain, J. D. Bate offers up this gem in describing Ishmael's character: He had a "wild and misanthropic disposition."[3]

Not only is the word "misanthropic" never used in any reasonably accurate translation of the Bible to describe Ishmael, but no word that could even approximate such definition as carried by this term is ever used. Why, then, do so many believers, leaders, and laypeople alike, share the same view as that put forth in the above passage? The reason is twofold.

First, to attempt to find specific reasons and catalysts for all modern events within Scripture, especially in the case of regions like the Middle East in which there have been so many situation-altering factors— population shifts, new religious dogmas, discoveries of oil, and the drawing of artificial but binding borders by European colonial powers, to name but a few – is a task doomed to failure at first initiation. Aside from the fact that such an effort defies logic and reason, it also is one attempting to utilize Scripture in a manner not intended or directed by those who received inspiration and wrote. Certainly Abraham made a serious blunder when he listened to Sarah's advice about their childlessness. The biblical narrative clearly reflects that mistake. However, the Bible is about redemption. The story of the graciousness of God permeates the book. No one should in the least be surprised that God has a marvelous plan for Abraham, Sarah, and Isaac, but also for Hagar and Ishmael. And there is much to be learned from the latter.

The second reason for the common misunderstanding of Ishmael among Christians, and generally the most prominent reason, lay in the

---

3 J. D. Bate, *An Examination of the Claims of Ishmael as Viewed by Muhammadans* (Banaras: E. J. Lazarus and Co., 1884), 167.

woefully errant interpretation of Genesis 16:12. Compounding the problem are numerous errors in translation among the many versions of Scripture now widely available. Regardless of levels of education or intellect, anyone attempting to interpret a passage of Scripture apart from an understanding of the mind-set and culture from which it came is on dangerous ground.

Having come down to comfort Hagar and to give her instruction and hope of a bright future because the "Lord has given heed to your affliction," the angel of the Lord then promises her that her descendants will be multiplied so that they will be too many to count (Genesis 16:10). He promised her the birth of a son whom she was to name, Ishmael (Genesis 16:11). The meaning of the name, Ishmael, is "God hears," for God had heard her cries of despair in the desert.

In Genesis 16:12, the angel then proceeds to tell her of the attributes and characteristics to be embodied by her son. "He will be a wild donkey of a man, his hand will be against everyone, and everyone's hand will be against him; and he will live to the east of all his brothers." Now, to modern western eyes and minds that seldom venture far from city centers or suburbs, to be called "a wild donkey of a man" will appear to be derogatory and revealing of a terribly flawed and, perhaps, dangerous man. To those finding beauty in the New York City skyline or the smog-shrouded, traffic-choked sprawl of greater Los Angeles, a wild donkey roaming upon the Arabian Desert may not be impressive. The man whose most cherished and most used personal possession is his top-of-the-line cellular phone, whose greatest conception of beauty is beheld in his flawless sports car, a man whose most intimidating conflicts have come in disputes with wife or girlfriend or whose boldest act of deterrence came in fighting off the eight-pound, loosed Pomeranian that nipped at his heels on the sidewalk may even see in "a wild donkey of a man" one who is unruly and misanthropic.

The problem with such a conclusion is that the wild donkey, in the eyes and minds of the people of the ancient Near East, was an animal of beauty to be admired for his strength, hardiness, resourcefulness, independence and love of a free-roaming life, disdain of civilization, and his resilience to becoming a beast of burden in servitude to men. Consider some of the Scripture references in which the characteristics of the wild donkey are admired or used as illustration (Job 38:9; 39:5-8; Jeremiah 2:24; and Hosea 8:9). To the people of the Bible, this was an animal to be esteemed and, in some respects, such as that in which some might covet the wings and vistas of an eagle, to be envied.

Such a perspective is not limited to the people of the Bible. A proverb of the Fulani people, who roam northern Africa from the Sudan in the east to Mauritania in the west, extols the animal with these words: "Love is a donkey freed of all tethers." All who have watched as a vigorous donkey, once freed of all packs, ropes, or reins, sprints away—sometimes bucking or kicking against the air—and then rolls pleasurably in the dust will understand well this African metaphor of love. Among most of the world's pastoral peoples, in fact, strength, hardiness, and independence are always admired, whether embodied by beast or man.

In the context of Abraham and Hagar's time and place, that Ishmael was to be "a wild donkey of a man" may be interpreted as both blessing and high praise. Ishmael would be strong and self-sufficient. He would be independent, shunning cities and settled lands while living off the harsh, wild country of the Arabian Desert where most feared to tread and few cared to dwell. He would live the free, ever-moving life of a nomad, and he would preserve his freedom through strength, wit, and skill. None would overtake him, defeat him, or put him into servitude.

That "his hand will be against everyone, and everyone's hand will be against him," is a statement that merely addresses the realities of nomadic life in virtually any region, and especially in the Arabian Desert.

There always have been levels of tension and mistrust among settled peoples and any nomadic groups that move on their margins. Some conflict, though variant in degree from infrequent to substantial, was inevitable. Further, there was generally inherent tension and competition among the various nomadic tribes themselves so that each of their hands, again in varying intensity and degree, was set against the hands of the others. This was surely the case among the Bedouin tribes of the Arabian Peninsula and actually prevailed until relatively recent years.

Further evidence of the esteem of the wild donkey in ancient Near Eastern eyes can be understood when considering what happened before and after the angel's appearance to Hagar. Before his appearance, she was fleeing virtually into the desert and toward sure death because of the oppression and affliction suffered under Sarah. After hearing from the angel what kind of man her promised son was to be, she willingly returned to Abraham's dwelling, only then content to bide her time and wait, knowing that freedom and security were to come.

Perseverance in Freedom

Those still wishing to assert that God, and perhaps Abraham also, were against Ishmael and Ishmael against them should consider three other passages. In Genesis 17:20, Abraham's love for Ishmael is made clear. After telling Abraham that the covenant of His chosen people would run through Isaac, God then says to him, "As for Ishmael, I have heard you." Nothing less than a genuine love, affection, and concern from father for son can be deduced from this. In prayer and in direct dialogue ("O that Ishmael might live before You!" Genesis 17:18), Abraham sought blessings and security for his firstborn son. God responded in love for Abraham and Ishmael: "Behold, I will bless him, and will make him fruitful and will multiply him exceedingly. He shall become the father of twelve princes, and I will make him a great nation."

Mysteries of the Bush

In Genesis 21:14-21, Abraham, yielding to Sarah's pressure after hearing an affirming word from God, turns Hagar and Ishmael out into the wilderness with a single water skin. When their water was gone and they sat down to die slowly, Hagar moved some distance away so as not to watch her son die. The author's terminology here is worthy of note. "Then she went and sat down opposite him, about a bowshot away...." As Hagar began to weep, the angel of the Lord called to her again. "What is the matter with you, Hagar? Do not fear, for God has heard the voice of the lad where he is. Arise, lift up the lad, and hold him by the hand, for I will make a great nation of him." Then God opened her eyes to a well from which both drank and filled their empty skin.

Not only did God hear Ishmael's cries, He responded, intervening directly to preserve the lives of him and his mother. Further, God then reiterated his promise that He would make Ishmael a great nation. Entailed in that promise was not merely survival, but rather a life of freedom, security, and plenty in an unforgiving land—a kind of life attainable only by a wild donkey of a man with the strength, hardiness, resourcefulness, wit, perseverance, and skills that such would demand.

Upon Sarah's death, Abraham took a second wife, Keturah, through whom he fathered more of the northern Arabian tribes through the six sons she bore to him. Abraham breathed his last at 175 years of age and was gathered to his people. Again, all who would assert the presence of a rift of hostility between Abraham and Isaac on the one side, and Ishmael on the other, should take note of Genesis 25:9. For there we are told that Isaac and Ishmael buried their father together in the cave of Machpelah. Further, there is nothing to suggest that the relationship between the two brothers was anything but peaceful.

Moreover, in the ardent monotheism that pervaded in the Arabian Peninsula for centuries after Abraham's death can be seen further evidence of Ishmael and his descendants as children of the covenant with the living God. As Tony Maalouf has aptly noted in his groundbreaking work, *Arabs in the Shadow of Israel*, idolatry on any significant scale did not begin to reappear in Arabia until much later, roughly coinciding with the time that such practices began to be common in Israel. Just as Ishmael carried the outer mark of the covenant of Abraham in his circumcision, so it would also appear that he held the inner mark of his father's faith.

Returning to the desert where the angel intervened to save the lives of Ishmael and Hagar with the water of the well, we move to Genesis 21:20. "God was with the lad, and he grew; and he lived in the wilderness and became an archer." *Archer* is sometimes translated as *bow hunter*, which here might be the better translation. For clearly, especially in the beginning, Ishmael would survive and live by his skills with bow and arrow, making him the first man in Scripture to be identified as a great bow hunter. Nimrod was singled out as a mighty hunter before the Lord, but we are told nothing of his choice of arms.

Ishmael was a shooter, undoubtedly taking many Arabian oryx, gazelles, roebuck, ibex and various other game with his powerful bow. Inherent in the fact is that God, in one way or another, gave Ishmael a knowledge of woods and the other organic materials of the desert and mountains necessary for the making and maintenance of bows and arrows. Too, God imparted to him the knowledge of wild country and an understanding of the wildlife therein, as both are requisite for a man to be able to live off a harsh and unforgiving land. We can see all of this implied in the phrase, "God was with the lad."

The phrase "and he grew" reveals that God imbued Ishmael with great strength, resilience, and an indomitable will. Without all, he would not have survived as a lad having to make his way and forge a home in the Arabian Desert. A bow, or any other weapon, especially prior to the advent of firearms, is only as good as the man who wields it.

God was with Ishmael and, in accordance with all that we are given in Scripture, Ishmael remained with God, holding to the faith of his father as he roamed the vast desert. Rather than following the errant course of common interpretations and seeing in Ishmael the antagonist to our faith, we should seek instead to focus on what is revealed to us in Scripture. "A wild donkey of a man," he was to be sure, a fact only appropriately understood and appreciated when taken in the ancient Near Eastern biblical context. As a wild donkey of a man, Ishmael was resilient, refusing to be daunted by extremes of heat, cold, hardship, hunger, or thirst. He was a provider and protector to his own, his deadly bow procuring the harvest of vital protein from wild game as efficiently as it was utilized for deterrent and defense against enemies. He was a lover of freedom, unwilling to submit himself or his own to the will or yoke of any man or nation. In it all, he adhered to the living God of his father.

Therein is left a facet of our spiritual heritage to be embraced and aspired by every Christian man. For we need not be nomads roaming freely on the desert to embody the virtues of Ishmael. To be resilient, holding the will to persevere through any hardship that comes; to provide and protect, using our skill at arms to feed, secure, and defend our own; and to cherish our freedom, being resolved to defend and maintain it at any cost are commitments that can be undertaken by all men possessed of the will and determination to do so.

The Gift of Freedom

Some will argue, as has become trendy now within certain circles, that freedom and liberty, so cherished by early Americans and their founding fathers, constitute a wholly secular objective that has no place in the gospel of Jesus Christ. While we will be among the first to assert that the ultimate objective of Jesus, who came to earth in Advent, had nothing to do with politics or the temporal liberties of men, we will also bring to light a few other facts. First, there are many closet socialists and other forms of leftists even within the church. Such men and women may present themselves as Christian pastors, scholars, writers, speakers, or leaders holding one expertise or another, speaking much of Jesus, of love (generally without substantial definition), of redistribution of wealth by force of law (in Jesus' name, of course), and the virtues of being nonjudgmental toward virtually any form of iniquity. Yet when you look only at what they do—what they attempt to bring to pass in society—most of it strangely seems to coincide with chief objectives of the political agenda of the secular left.

Most avid hunters pronounce who they are and what they believe with honesty and forthright clarity. They cherish their freedoms and will do all that they can to maintain them. They believe in big guns, strong bows, sharp arrows, long spears, a keen edge on sword and knife, big trucks, small guns, substantial ammo reserves, fast horses, and faster camels. We join them but also add a strong commitment to the inerrancy of the entire Word of God and strive to obey all commands and embody all principles therein. On the other hand, closet leftists, wherever they insert themselves, seldom make a statement of where they stand or what they wish to accomplish. The absence of clear, straightforward honesty, integrity, and clarity likely reveals the nature of their objectives as well as the lack of the actual substance of their faith.

Second, with regard to freedom, there is obviously no biblical prohibition to having liberty or enjoying its fruits, though some even within Christendom surely seem to insinuate that there is. Further, there is no mandate to give up any freedom that may be possessed. Nor is there any prohibition, within clearly set parameters, of doing all that you can to protect and preserve freedom.

Only by the allowances and fruits of freedom have significant numbers of missionaries been sent into all of the world to impart the gospel of Christ. Only with some measure of freedom can we worship openly, preach the gospel, and speak as we wish. Only with the profits and securities of freedom can charitable deeds and organizations flourish. You need only to see how many charitable groups have been initiated in North Korea, China, or Iran to realize as much. How many missionaries have gone out from such countries to carry the gospel? What is the status there of freedom of speech and religious practice? What of their medical facilities and the security of their lives and property?

Many have faithfully followed Christ while living in bondage or, at least, without most of the freedoms that we in America have enjoyed. Nevertheless, the fact does not constitute either a mandate or an excuse for eschewing or failing to try to preserve the liberty that we have. That Ishmael enjoyed and preserved his freedom and, even more telling, that God, in fact, gave that freedom to him as a component of His rich blessings upon Abraham and his descendants, should serve as a reminder that any freedoms we have are a gift from God—a gift not to be taken lightly or for granted.

To cherish and protect our freedom, then, and to build strength, resilience, skill at arms, and skill in the hunt—all while adhering to our faith—is to embrace and to act upon the legacy and heritage passed down to us through the covenant of Abraham by Ishmael. Other men of the Bible contributed to that heritage, but for none are the words of Scripture so revealing regarding the value of the hunt and the freedom to be enjoyed in the hardy life amid pursuits in wild country. A mighty hunter before the Lord, by our understanding, is a man strong, proficient in arms, and skilled in the hunt who keeps before him always the will and ways of the Lord. Ishmael, from what is given through Scripture, was all of that. Every man, holding the requisite commitment, determination, and will, can be the same.

Hunting and Life

THE LEGACY OF JOB

Job, as previously noted, also was a man who knew wild country and all varieties of critters very well. We may also presume that the righteous Arab sheikh, "a blameless and upright man" of whom there were none like him on the earth, was always up for a good hunt. For it is from his beautiful, poetic work—perhaps the oldest book in the Bible—that we learn of one of the most riveting hunting stories never told (never told in print, that is, though surely relived by all involved over many a warming fire in the Arabian night). What proves most interesting is how and when the story comes up and, not least, who brought it up.

Job lived in the land of Uz. Although scholars cannot establish with certainty the specific location of Uz, we are safe in presuming a region in northern Arabia with the possibility of an extension as far north as Hauran, still well south of Damascus. Job may have been a contemporary of Abraham or even preceded him a bit. Some have argued for placing Job within the patriarchal period but well after Abraham, thus making him and his friends, who came in his time of sickness and loss, descendants of Ishmael. The pervasive monotheism evident in their exchange could be seen as evidence for a later date. The specifics of dating the matter are not for our purposes. All that needs to be understood is that what transpired happened a very long time ago, and we can be certain that Uz was wild country at the time. There was much to hunt; and because there was much to hunt, Job's massive domestic herds and flocks had to be protected day and night.

At the time our story comes up, many years had likely passed, and Job had grown older and wiser. One or two lessons, at least, seem to have come from this particular hunt. Perhaps it was a fishing trip that turned into a hunting trip because of what unexpectedly broke the surface of the water. With the information given, we cannot be sure. Nevertheless, even as the wise and righteous sheikh remembered and relived the adventure with his companions in the still silence of the desert nights, he likely never realized that therein were still more lessons to be learned. He surely could not have foreseen the circumstances under which the incident would be recalled by an outside party, let alone who that party was to be.

Job's Circumstances and Questions

The circumstances were those of extreme suffering. Job, unbeknownst to him, had become a participant in what, even at that early date, was already a long-running battle between Satan and God—a part of the ongoing clash between evil and good that rages behind all that is visible and tangible still today. Satan had been allowed to test Job—to afflict him horribly in the belief that Job, the most righteous man on earth, would then blame, curse, and turn away from God. Yet Job, though suffering terribly, did not blame or curse God. Nevertheless, he did wonder and he did ask questions just as most of us would do, at the least, in similar circumstances.

Job's friends were certainly theists, and almost all of what they had to say was theologically correct. But a man suffering with a toothache will not be pleased to know that the dentist pulled the wrong tooth even if he did it according to the latest insights into the treatment of bicuspids and is proud of his evident expertise. The problem was not their theology. It was their lack of discernment. Assuming the worst about Job and about God (i.e., that all maladies must be God's punishment for wrong), they misapplied good theology to the wrong individual.

Job had lost his children to seeming natural disaster. Many of his servants had been murdered, and much of his livestock—and thus his wealth—had been taken away by marauding desert tribes. Then his own health had been taken, as he was severely and painfully physically afflicted. There was pain, confusion, hurt, sorrow, sadness, longing, and anger in varying combinations and degrees as Job sought the counsel and comfort of friends and searched for reasons and answers for the inexplicable tragedy that had overtaken him.

Having seen Job's suffering, having heard his questions and prayers, and having listened to the voices and opinions of Job's friends, God finally emerges from a whirlwind at the beginning of chapter 38 and commences a conversation with a question that remains one of the greatest lines in history. Referring to the opinions voiced by Job's friends, God asks, "Who is this that darkens counsel by words without knowledge?" He then proceeds through the next four chapters to answer Job's questions regarding his suffering and loss without a single reference to the tangible issues at hand and in Job's mind—all of which, of course, related to the tragedy and hardship he had endured and the reasons for it.

God's Interrogation of Job

Job's questions, instead, were answered by a litany of questions from God Himself regarding the mystery, magnificence, and majesty of all creation. They were questions meant to highlight, for Job and for us, the unfathomable and unassailable power that brought all things into being and the force that moves, holds, and keeps in harmony all elements of nature. In the numerous references to the magnificence, strength, speed, and durability of particular animals, Job, like us, was reminded then of the only creative intellect and inscrutable power that could design and sustain such amazing and beautiful creatures:

"Where were you when I laid the foundation of the earth? . . .
Who set its measurements? . . .

"Or *who* enclosed the sea with doors
When, bursting forth, it went out from the womb[?] . . .
"Have you ever in your life commanded the morning,
And caused the dawn to know its place[?] . . .

Mysteries of the Bush

"Have you entered into the springs of the sea
Or walked in the recesses of the deep?
"Have the gates of death been revealed to you,
Or have you seen the gates of deep darkness? . . .

"Where is the way to the dwelling of light? . . .
"Have you entered the storehouses of the snow,
Or have you seen the storehouses of the hail[?] . . .
"Who has cleft a channel for the flood,
Or a way for the thunderbolt[?] . . .
"Can you bind the chains of the Pleiades[?] . . .
"Can you lead forth a constellation in its season,
And guide the Bear with her satellites? . . .
"Can you lift up your voice to the clouds,
So that an abundance of water will cover you? . . .
"Who has put wisdom in the innermost being
Or given understanding to the mind? . . .
"Can you hunt the prey for the lion,
Or satisfy the appetite of the young lions[?] . . .
"Do you give the horse *his* might?
Do you clothe his neck with a mane? . . .
"Is it by your understanding that the hawk soars,
Stretching his wings toward the south?
"Is it at your command that the eagle mounts up
And makes his nest on high . . .
Upon the rocky crag, an inaccessible place[?] . . .

"Behold now, Behemoth, which I made as well as you;
He eats grass like an ox.
"Behold now, his strength in his loins
And his power in the muscles of his belly.
"He bends his tail like a cedar;
The sinews of his thighs are knit together.

"His bones are tubes of bronze;
His limbs are like bars of iron" (from Job 38–40).[4]

That God chose this description of the hippopotamus to remind Job of His own power and creative intellect at this point in their dialogue may seem surprising to some. Yet any who have had a close encounter with an agitated hippo in the wild, seen the utter destruction he can very quickly wreak on the human body, seen him run (yes, hippos are very fast on a short charge), or examined the skin, bones, muscle and teeth on a dead hippo will not be surprised. Some may wonder: Why not use a lion here instead? Well, I have seen a hippo back down a 500-pound lion. Aside from being the number one killer of humans in Africa every year (causing more fatalities even than lions, leopards, crocodiles, elephants, buffalo or hyenas), they are simply one of the most powerful and formidable creatures in the world. Their mouths are like an old-style Samsonite suitcase full of sharpened ivory teeth. They are dangerous to hunt even with a rifle; but in the eras before firearms, let alone in Job's time, any encounter with hippos was perilous.

A Hunt for Hippos

Maybe my most terrifying moment on a hunt involved a relatively young but large hippo. Finding a place along Lake Kariba between Zambia and Zimbabwe where hippos were obviously nesting for the evening, we approached eight-foot-high reeds with narrow paths created by the movement of these giants. Though spooky enough edging through the reeds, neither hippo nor pod (a grouping of hippos) was discovered. Pausing to recover breath at the edge of the lake in what we were positive was only inches deep, the professional hunter, my son-in-law Mark Howell, and I spoke quietly, rifles at our sides. Big mistake! From nowhere, suddenly the enormous head, neck,

---

4 From Job 38:4-5, 8, 12, 16-17, 19, 22, 25, 31-32, 34, 36, 39; 39:19, 26, 28; 40:15-18.

and front legs of a teenage hippo rose from what was obviously greater depth than we knew. He was so close that I could have touched his head. By the time I was in hasty retreat, he returned to the water. Mark's gentle, unnecessary, and somewhat flattering remark was, "Hey, Dad, I had no idea that a 63-year-old man could move that fast."

Egyptian soldiers used to hunt hippos on the banks of the Nile. They did so for several reasons. First, hippos, with their substantial appetites, were destructive to crops, as they would come up onto the banks at night and eat their fill. Second, they were dangerous and took a heavy toll on human life then just as they do now. Third, their ample meat is quite tasty and provided a welcome supplement to the average soldier's mundane and sometimes sparse daily diet. Fourth, as most of these soldiers were young men, they took up the hunt for the challenge and action it brought. The challenge, though, was one only taken by a large number of soldiers wielding spears and harpoons, and for good reason. One or even a few men with spears would have stood very little chance of survival after the first spear struck, especially if there were no easily climbed trees nearby.

Job's Hunt for Leviathan

Nevertheless, the description of the hippo, the other magnificent creatures, and of the incomprehensible power that formed and sustains the universe were but a prelude to the climax to which God was going in this predominantly one-sided dialogue. Where He was going was to a reminiscence of the spectacular but ultimately unsuccessful hunt; the day long before when Job and his companions decided to try to get their harpoons and spears into the vitals of Leviathan. Much time may have passed, but God knew well that it had been an experience that no hunter could have forgotten.

Hunting and Life

And so God came to the point (Job 41:1-34):

"Can you draw out Leviathan with a fishhook?
Or press down his tongue with a cord?
"Can you put a rope in his nose
Or pierce his jaw with a hook?
"Will he make many supplications to you,
Or will he speak to you soft words?
"Will he make a covenant with you?
Will you take him for a servant forever?
"Will you play with him as with a bird,
Or will you bind him for your maidens?
"Will the traders bargain over him?
Will they divide him among the merchants?
"Can you fill his skin with harpoons,
Or his head with fishing spears?
"Lay your hand on him;
Remember the battle; you will not do it again!
"Behold, your expectation is false;
Will you be laid low even at the sight of him?
"No one is so fierce that he dares to arouse him;
Who then is he that can stand before Me?
"Who has given to Me that I should repay *him*?
Whatever is under the whole heaven is Mine.

"I will not keep silence concerning his limbs,
Or his mighty strength, or his orderly frame.
"Who can strip off his outer armor?
Who can come within his double mail?
"Who can open the doors of his face?
Around his teeth there is terror.
"*His* strong scales are *his* pride,

Mysteries of the Bush

Shut up *as with* a tight seal.
"One is so near to another
That no air can come between them.
"They are joined one to another;
They clasp each other and cannot be separated.
"His sneezes flash forth light,
And his eyes are like the eyelids of the morning.
"Out of his mouth go burning torches;
Sparks of fire leap forth.
"Out of his nostrils smoke goes forth
As *from* a boiling pot and *burning* rushes.
"His breath kindles coals,
And a flame goes forth from his mouth.
"In his neck lodges strength,
And dismay leaps before him.
"The folds of his flesh are joined together,
Firm on him and immovable.
"His heart is as hard as a stone,
Even as hard as a lower millstone.
"When he raises himself up, the mighty fear;
Because of the crashing they are bewildered.
"The sword that reaches him cannot avail,
Nor the spear, the dart or the javelin.
"He regards iron as straw,
Bronze as rotten wood.
"The arrow cannot make him flee;
Slingstones are turned into stubble for him.
"Clubs are regarded as stubble;
He laughs at the rattling of the javelin.
"His underparts are *like* sharp potsherds;
He spreads out *like* a threshing sledge on the mire.

"He makes the depths boil like a pot;
He makes the sea like a jar of ointment.
"Behind him he makes a wake to shine;
One would think the deep to be gray-haired.
"Nothing on earth is like him,
One made without fear.
"He looks on everything that is high;
He is king over all the sons of pride."

The identity of Leviathan is a mystery and likely will remain so this side of heaven. After we have crossed the last river, though, we plan on quickly finding Job and hearing the whole story of the thrilling hunt gone wrong. The most common view is that Job makes use of the mythology of the ancients and that Leviathan is hypothetical. Although a hypothetical Leviathan is possible even without harming the text of Scripture, it is not likely. Such a conclusion is hardly necessary and is notably different for Bible authors. Another common view holds that Leviathan was a Nile crocodile. This is certainly possible. Hunting in crocodile-infested waters with rifles even today is very dangerous. The animals are difficult to kill, and their recovery is more difficult, due largely to their constant proximity to murky water. They are extremely powerful, lightning quick, and chillingly stealthy. Once while camped on the Zambezi River, I asked a local pastor if he personally knew of anyone having been killed by a croc. With a gesture mingling disgust with a reluctant submission to fate, he replied, "I've lost two church members to crocodiles just this year."

For Job and his companions to have landed spears and harpoons into a Nile crocodile surely could have resulted in a hunt and battle never to be forgotten. For having indicated that at least some of the spears and harpoons gained penetration, though none apparently with sufficient depth to pierce vitals, God reveals that He knows well Job's disposition on the matter. "Remember the battle; you will not do it again!" (Job 41:8).

Yet the whole of the text in chapter 41 suggests the possibility and, in our view, the probability, that Leviathan was actually a creature larger and far more formidable than the greatest of Nile crocodiles:

"Who can strip off his outer armor?
Who can come within his double mail? . . .
"Who can open the doors of his face?
"*His* strong scales are *his* pride,
Shut up *as with* a tight seal.
"One is so near to another
That no air can come between them. . . .
"His sneezes flash forth light,
And his eyes are like the eyelids of the morning.
"Out of his mouth go burning torches;
Sparks of fire leap forth. . . .
"His breath kindles coals,
And a flame goes forth from his mouth. . . .
"His underparts are *like* sharp potsherds . . .
"He makes the depths boil like a pot;
He makes the sea like a jar of ointment.
"Behind him he makes a wake to shine;
One would think the deep to be gray-haired.
"Nothing on earth is like him . . . .[5]

Crocodiles are formidable enough, but Leviathan appears to be something far more powerful and fearsome. Could the allusions to fire be merely metaphor? Absolutely they could, but then there still is the double-mail; the hard, sharp outward-jutting scales on his belly; and the notable wake he leaves behind as he swims. Remember that

---

5 From Job 41: 13, 15-16, 18-19, 21, 30-33.

Hunting and Life

Job is possibly the oldest book of Scripture and that his days may have pre-dated Abraham. We do not and cannot know with certainty what creatures may have lived upon the earth then but passed into extinction relatively shortly thereafter.

Scientists and other experts assure us that all dinosaurs, and essentially any creatures resembling them, had long been extinct by Job's time. However, just in this past year, I have seen articles on and photographs of at least four living species that scientists and experts had pronounced extinct. One of them, of all things, was a quite large tortoise living on a small island close to South America! I am not sure quite how they missed this one for so many years. Tortoises are not exactly known for speed or skills of evasion, and on an island no less! The point to be taken is that scientists and so-called "experts" do not even know with certainty all of the creatures that inhabit the earth and the seas today. Discoveries of new species and rediscoveries of others said to have been extinct are tantamount to a frank admission of the fact on their part. If any expert cannot tell you for certain what is and is not living upon the land and in the water right now, even with the substantial funding and technology available to him, then do not worry too much about what they proclaim to have existed or not existed four thousand or more years ago.

For those who would assert their surety that fire-spitting beasts, such as the dragons of many legends, are merely the fantasies of the imaginations of men, consider the case of the Bombardier beetle. This diminutive ground beetle can be found on almost every continent. The name is derived from the unique defense mechanism they possess. When threatened, they are able to discharge a burning hot, corrosive chemical spray from their abdominal tip. Some species can direct their spray in various directions. Stored chemical compounds that mix with water and catalytic enzymes cause heating and the creation of gas, which then prompts the powerful expulsion of the burning spray. The spray is lethal to attacking insects and other small creatures and can cause painful burns on human skin. Since we have a multitude of beetles less than an inch long designed to carry nature's fully operational Zippo lighters on their backsides as they roam among us (any discussions on how this mechanism evolved should prove enlightening), it would not seem far-fetched to suggest that the same Creator who designed them also made greater creatures with mechanisms similar but in capacities to match their greater proportions, and that it may well have been some such critter that Job made the mistake of harpooning on the open water.

Job's hunt-turned-battle-for-survival may have occurred on the blue, clear water of the Red Sea. Perhaps it happened even further from his pastoral home. Adventurous men have always been inclined to travel far, especially when there is the prospect of hunting formidable game.

What holds inescapably riveting, though, is that in response to Job's questions regarding the reasons for his suffering, God addressed neither his suffering nor the reasons for it. Rather, He reminded him of a hunting trip gone awry, using the strength, solidity, and prowess—all far surpassing the capacities of any man—of an animal designed by His mind and made by His hands to remind Job and all who would follow of His omnipotence, omnipresence, and unceasing sovereignty.

God's Lessons for Job

To ascertain all that God is saying to Job and to us through these four chapters, culminating in the recounting of the hunt for Leviathan, we must do some reading between the lines while keeping in mind the entirety of the context of the whole book. Then upon considering what was said as well as what was not said, we might discern the essence of God's primary points of learning to be as follows (Armour's paraphrase of this passage from Job):

> *There is much for you to learn and to understand just by looking around, above, and below you. Consider the sun, moon, and stars.*

Hunting and Life

Ponder the depths, vastness, and mystery of the seas and all life therein. Contemplate the mountains, the rivers that wind and flow down to the sea, the rain, snow, hail, and the power of the great tempests. Do you know by what power such hang, stand, flow, move, or are contained? Can you demonstrate the same power?

What of My creatures? Their strength, beauty, majesty, and understanding? Do you provide the abundance of which they all eat? Do you give them their understanding of how to procure their food or of how to find or build their lodging? Can you match the strength and speed of the great among them?

O, but you hunt! Then you will understand more, for to the man who is diligent and observes well, there is much of life to be learned and understood on the hunt. But a fraction of the power at My fingertips you have felt at Leviathan's pull against your spears and cords, as the crocodile submerged with your harpoons, and as Behemoth's jaws closed upon your boat and then on your companion's leg. You felt it in the power of the horse between your knees and in the speed of the wind between his ears. You experienced My genius when you tried but failed to ascend to the nest of the black eagle, his dwelling high upon the cliff and accessible only to him and to his own. Too, in the muscles, bones, and vitals of the creatures you have opened up, did you not also find the creative genius of My mind and the power of My hand there as well?

The power that formed and sustains all of these things is the same power that still rules the universe, the earth, and all creatures therein. By this power you are held, guided, and protected—now and for always. There is no power that can snatch you from My hand.

While there is much that you can learn and understand, there also is much that you cannot know or understand. There is much that you cannot see. The battle between evil and good is far older than are you, and it is much bigger than the span and happenings within your life. The battle raged long before you emerged from the womb and will continue well after you are gone until My time and purposes are fulfilled.

If you suffer, then you must persevere in faith and righteousness, knowing that the power that formed Behemoth and Leviathan is the power that will hold, protect, and sustain you. The knowledge from which came sun, moon, stars, mountains, rivers, springs, and sea is the knowledge that pierces through to your own heart and mind and knows at all times what is best for you. My eyes, which behold all things at all times—seeing all that is invisible to you—are upon you and your family always.

Job, in his wisdom and in his understanding as a hunter, fisherman, and observer of nature, demonstrated his discernment and understanding of all these things. When God finishes His reminiscence of the hunt for Leviathan, Job opens chapter 42 in confession and complete submission to whatever would be the will of his God:

Then Job answered the LORD AND SAID,

"I know that You can do all things,
And that no purpose of Yours can be thwarted.
'Who is this that hides counsel without knowledge?'
Therefore I have declared that which I did not understand,
Things too wonderful for me, which I did not know."
'Hear, now, and I will speak;
I will ask You, and You instruct me.'
"I have heard of You by the hearing of the ear;
But now my eye sees You;
Therefore I retract,
And I repent in dust and ashes" (vv. 1-6).

Job saw God not because they stood face to face but because he saw Him in the process of contemplating His questions regarding His creation and in his remembrance of the great hunt for Leviathan. He recognized God in the overwhelming evidence of creative genius all around him and understood that far more was ultimately at stake than the mere events within his own sojourn under the sun was happening.

Upon hearing Job's confession, God rebuked Job's friends for their errant assessments of the reasons for his suffering. He then healed Job's body and restored his wealth, increasing it twofold over what Job had previously. Finally, He gave Job and his wife seven sons and three daughters and allowed him to live for 140 years so that he saw his sons and grandsons down to four generations.

The Success of God's Teaching Method

God's unconventional method of addressing Job's struggle and questions was so successful for two reasons. First, as a natural outdoorsman and hunter, Job understood much that simply is not readily or easily comprehended by people who have never encountered wildlife wholly on its terms in truly wild country (i.e., not in zoos or heavily visited game parks). In the captivity of zoos or the manufactured, false environments created at most game reserves, animal behavior changes. Only in truly wild country where all predators hunt (man included) and all prey is wary can animal behavior in its wholly natural form be observed. Furthermore, until you have directly challenged the strength of a powerful animal in some way or form, you simply cannot fully appreciate the power, endurance, and quickness they have. Intellectual knowledge is seldom equal to the raw understanding attained by experience.

Second, God's method of dialogue, brought to a climax with the reminder of Leviathan, was successful because of the fact that hunting is one of the best tools and methods by which to teach some of the most vital and valuable lessons of life. While the hunt is always an ideal setting for the mentoring and teaching of boys and young men by older men, neither gender nor age constitute any barrier to lessons that may be learned or understanding that can be acquired.

Job, after all, was long past the days of youth and was wiser and more discerning than most men—if not all—at the time when God chose to use a hunt to teach him a lesson and to broaden his understanding. Chief among the factors that make hunting an effective method by which to teach lessons of life is the fact that hunting is generally a lot like life.

Solomon expresses this truth: "A lazy man does not roast his prey, but the precious possession of a man is diligence" (Proverbs 12:27). The analogy chosen by the wise king here is clearly one of the hunt as the word "prey" negates the roasting of a lamb or goat. The lazy hunter, especially in challenging terrain and in pursuit of the more elusive game, will not be roasting any prey taken by the weapons of his hands. So it is in life. If you do not prepare your mind and body properly, receive wise counsel, and push yourself relentlessly and diligently toward your objective, then you are unlikely to achieve much success.

The Value of Diligence

Sometimes you may be uncertain of your objective in life. I was so coming out of high school and then even upon graduation from college. In Psalm 37:4-5, David wrote,

> Delight yourself in the Lord;
> And He will give you the desires of your heart.
> Commit your way to the Lord,
> Trust also in Him, and He will do it.

This should not be taken as a promise that God will give you all that you desire. Rather, it is a promise that, if you honor the Lord in your heart and in your actions—that is, to commit your way to Him—then He will show you the true desires of your heart of which He will have given

Hunting and Life

you the abilities and capacities to achieve and to gain. Being influenced by the counsel and ways of this world, we often may not know the true desires of our hearts, or we may lose sight of them. When we trust in the Lord and strive to walk in His ways, however, He will guide us to the place we need to be and to the tasks to which we must set our hands. Only in that place and devoted to these tasks, whatever they may be, will we then truly discover the innermost desires of our hearts and find complete fulfillment and sublime peace passing all comprehension.

A crucial component in committing your way to the Lord is the diligence of which Solomon wrote. Diligence, of course, includes our adherence to the precepts and principles of Scripture, but it also entails the preparation of our minds and bodies so as to be ready for whatever may come. This means that we push ourselves hard, pursuing with all of our strength, energy, and ingenuity all tasks or occupations to which we set our hands. Ultimately, then, our way and our course will be made clear.

Paths of Discovery

In hunting, as in life, you sometimes do not know specifically what you are after or exactly where you will be going. My first hunt in the East African country of Tanzania was much this way. We knew little of the country and terrain. Although we knew about some of the game, there was much about which we knew nothing from among around twenty-five different kinds of animals that we could take. Furthermore, our hunt would not be led by professionals but by local missionaries.

Our resolve then was simply that we would push hard and hunt long and see where our journey led us. The result was that, as we pressed hard and searched across the beautiful, wild savannah, the desires of our hearts were made known to us. Not only did we see some of the most lovely country upon God's earth and animal herds in varieties and numbers such as we had never seen before, but we also took eight animals in less than a week of hunting. Some, as is usually the case, proved elusive, such as the vaunted Cape buffalo and the regal Lesser Kudu. Yet with the game we took and prepared, we returned home with some splendid trophies; and, more important, missionaries and the local Baptist seminary students, who had little money, were left with freezers full of lean, organic protein. For in that part of northern Tanzania, the game taken on safari was the only consistent source of meat, let alone good meat, for these students and their families. Better than the trophies, too, were the lifelong friends made and the bond of a wonderful experience that would live in our hearts and memories forever.

Intentional Pursuits

Usually, when hunting, you do know what you are after. Nevertheless, in hunting just as in the pursuits of life, you do not know where, when, or if you will find it. This fact of the hunt is one that makes the quest and the challenge so riveting and irresistible to many men and women. Even when you know the animals and the country well, there is no guarantee of success. This is why it is called "hunting." The true hunter wants not a mere kill or any guarantee thereof, but he desires the journey, the pursuit, and the challenge.

I once hunted Greater Kudu specifically and relentlessly for five full days. On foot, hands and knees, and on my belly I tried to locate a good bull and get positioned for a shot in the thick bushveld of Zimbabwe. Following my professional hunter's lead, I saw several very nice bulls but was never able to get a good enough look to shoot. Every time the situation appeared promising, something happened. Sometimes it was the heavy brush or a shift in the wind. On one occasion our path was being cut off in the long grass by the unexpected appearance of an agitated and extremely large Black Mamba. Twice it was the sounding of the alarm known well to southern African game—the call of the notorious "go-away" bird.

Success in the pursuit of kudu began to appear unlikely since I had few days left to hunt. Late one afternoon, the professional hunter suggested that we go shoot an impala—a common animal there—for camp meat. We had not gone far from camp when, most unexpectedly, it happened. A magnificent kudu bull broke through the brush and, seeing or winding us, stopped in his tracks. He held still but for a couple of seconds as I quickly shouldered the .375 H&H Magnum, then sprung for the nearest cover, but the pause—likely by but fractions of a second—had been just long enough.

Readiness for Risks

You can know what you want to find, but you can never know for sure how, where, or when opportunity will come. For this reason, in hunting as in life, you must be diligent in preparation and pursuit and then always be ready. Often, in hunting with due diligence served you will find what is sought in the place and under the conditions in which you could reasonably expect it to be found. Seemingly just as often, however, we have returned to favored locations seeking deer or elk and found none, only then to have them appear at a place and time where we would not have thought it likely. Opportunities and relationships in other facets of our lives have followed the same pattern.

Son-in-law Mark Howell had his own unique experience with a kudu. "First" was a tracker, so named by his mother who bore him, well . . . first. Our professional hunter (P.H.) was involved in a negotiation on the phone and so gave First the opportunity of a lifetime. "You act like a P.H. and take Mark to find a kudu." First desperately wished to succeed in this endeavor. Sure enough, across the bluff above them walked several kudus, one of which was a really nice bull. First pointed and nodded. Boom! And down he went. Now Mark was excited, but not anything like as much as First. Running up the ridge, First piled on the still thrashing 750-pound animal at considerable risk to himself. "First has his first!" he shouted, grinning from ear to ear.

Mysteries of the Bush

Hunting is like life in that there always is danger. The danger increases commensurate with the terrain, weather, and critters present in a given locale. Parts of Africa are home to substantially more hazards than in Texas or Alaska; yet there are plenty of critters or situations in Alaska and Texas that can send you to the hospital—or worse. We have made numerous trips to medical clinics—or at least what passed for such—during hunts through the years. We once had to carry a very heavy hunter for nearly a mile following a lower leg injury in a desert canyon.

For the sake of an ever-softening society and culture that is obsessed with safety, longevity, and the varied pursuits of the modern fountain of eternal youth, let us share with you the single most dangerous thing you can ever do. The act is one that often leads to injury and always and invariably to death. The act is called "living." What is even more perilous is living to the fullest—getting away from the front of the television and computer, shunning the mall, avoiding the so-called "fast life" (a misnomer if ever there was one) in trendy clubs, limiting your time in the fashionable coffee houses with complimentary Wi-Fi, and abstaining, men, from frivolous activities with your female friends that might demonstrate how sensitive and open-minded you are.

Living is dangerous and always terminal. Yet life is the gift given us by God, and we are meant to live it fully with diligence, effort, and purpose just as the great men and women of the Bible lived their lives. For men who would follow Jesus Christ and live by the principles and precepts of Scripture, what should matter is not merely that you live but, rather, how you live. To take pointless and unnecessary risks or to behave with carelessness in any situation is not what is recommended or praised here. But to challenge yourself intellectually, spiritually, and physically—actions that, generally, in one way or another will lead to some form of calculated and necessary risk—is essential in establishing the whole of biblical manhood.

A Sense of Humor

In hunting just as in all aspects of life, all kinds of things will happen. Bad things will happen. Good things will happen. Strange and sometimes inexplicable things happen. Invariably, some absolutely hilarious things will happen. Boys and young men will laugh at the mishaps of others, but they will also eventually be forced to laugh at themselves. Never underestimate the value of this. Life is more productive, not to mention a lot more enjoyable, when you keep all of your senses sharp, especially your sense of humor.

I laughed at my father when he missed an easy shot or tumbled down a canyon. Then one day I had a perfect shot on a fine Thompson's gazelle standing broadside. The problem was that at the report of my Remington, the buck with the tall horns did not move, but the small hornless female behind him dropped like a sack of potatoes. Once I got over my anger, and realizing that the ribbing, which began right then and there, would be with me for a lifetime—and I do still hear about it even thirty years later—I laughed about it, too. The problem is that when that unseen doe collapsed, it so repulsed Armour that I was nearly killed when, laughing, I fell off the top of the truck on which I was lying while looking through binoculars. I still cannot figure out how his bullet did that or how I survived the fall.

When my friend Jason was told that he kept missing deer because he was flinching in anticipation of his rifle's recoil but vigorously denied that he would ever flinch, someone got his rifle and subtly removed the chambered cartridge. Then when the next deer appeared and his rifle barrel jumped about three inches as his hammer clicked on an empty chamber he knew that he had been caught in front of all of us. Once he got over his anger, he, too, laughed at himself, having learned one lesson on hunting and a more subtle one on life.

Ranchers Freida Kay and Jerry Davenport, taught us so much about the flora and fauna of the west. Freida Kay domesticated a small buck and a javelina and had a remarkable touch with all critters. My wife Dorothy has her Ph.D. from the University of South Africa, but we also got more than university educations at the tutoring of trackers with little or no formal education. We love them all, but the Ndebeles are my favorites. Possessed of a great sense of humor, they love what happens on the hunt. As a reasonably old man, I was disembarking from our hunting vehicle and missed the second of five steps down. Lying at the foot of a considerable hill down which I had plummeted, rifle and all, I first checked to see what was broken. Fortunately, only my pride. Looking to the truck, I saw no trackers. They were, it turned out, in the bottom of the truck laughing to such an extent that they could not stand.

On another occasion, I chased an army of baboons for nearly five miles trying to get a shot. Breathless, I took careful aim at a nice male and squeezed the trigger. The fear of every hunter had come to pass. No round in the chamber! And that in the company of about eight people who could scarcely contain themselves and made little attempt to do so. Roils of laughter sent the baboons screeching on their way. Two more miles and we caught up. All the trackers knew that I was a preacher, so they found it again hysterical when my big male, just as I took aim, decided that it was the appropriate time and place to procreate new baboons! I could not shoot, much to the chorus of laughter and slapping of backs on the part of the trackers!

To relate all of the funny, crazy, and outright strange things that have happened on our numerous hunts is not possible here. Likely such an undertaking would equal in length a book in and of itself. When you take a group of strong, spirited, and determined men and boys pitted against stronger animals possessed of an equal determination to evade, eat, mate, defend, and survive, you then have a potent mix for the living cocktail of the good, the bad, the ugly, the strange, and the hilarious. Then throw in inclement and unpredictable weather, challenging-to-

Hunting and Life

outright-treacherous terrain, formidable critters that have nothing to do with you and the quarry you seek and yet may show up with bad intentions anyway, an array of potent weaponry, and, in some locales, the presence of indigenous tribes still living as they have for hundreds of years or more. With that, the cocktail ingredients surge beyond the makings of a strong double to a punch bowl full!

All of these ingredients are a part of every life lived. There will always be the good, bad, ugly, crazy, inexplicably strange, and the humorous. There is no better school and field study for the young to be taught of these realities of life and how to deal with them than that provided on the hunt.

Encounters with Crafty Crooks

For any still unsure of whether or not truth, in fact, is both stranger and more interesting than fiction, we will let the volatile but always thrilling cocktail of the hunt rest with this. Two hyenas killed and ate more than fifty people in the Mlanje District of Malawi in the late 1950s. When a hunter named Balestra finally hunted them down and killed them, the two powerful man-eaters were found to be wearing beaded necklaces, and one of them had on a pair of khaki shorts! Now, consider this in light of the commonly held belief among numerous African tribes that hyenas are often the pets of witches, and that the witches, through their magical powers, can use the hyenas to carry out their malevolent bidding.

Furthermore, a Zambian professional hunter and friend, Pete Fisher, has had several strange experiences with hyenas over the years. Sufficiently strange and inexplicable that he once told me his strong belief that "the hyena is an animal that we have not yet fully understood." Inherent to that observation, he would also agree that the workings of evil—African witchcraft among them—are yet to be understood and likely never will be.

Once, when hunting in the Luangwa River region of Zambia, a situation developed such that, in Pete's words, "I had no choice. I had to do something." Meat from previously taken game, and quite a lot of it, was being pilfered from the tent that served as the camp kitchen. That hyenas had been sneaking into camp at night was evident enough in the tracks left behind. Yet the boldness and audacity of these intruders, as well as the volume of meat taken, suggested to the Zambian camp staff something other than hyenas, notorious camp menaces though they had always been. The camp staff and trackers, presuming that theft so deft and on such a scale could only be the work of humans, began to accuse each other of stealing the meat. Accusations and arguments escalated, and it was not long before Pete was on the verge of having a brawl in his camp. For that reason he had to take action, simultaneously putting an end to the theft while proving to his staff that all had been the mischief of a few hyenas.

So Pete, with rifle and spotlight, picked a spot just outside camp and sat up through the night. Sure enough, in the dark, silent hours deep into the night, he spotted the unmistakable shapes of two hyenas closing on the kitchen tent. When he started to move and put the spotlight on them, they ran, at which point Pete and some of his trackers took to the Land Rover and gave chase. With the powerful light giving them advantage, they followed the critters easily and kept close. Pete, though perhaps a bit surprised, was glad to see that the hyenas then took a course from which there could be no escape.

The bank of the river over which the two hyenas vanished was high and steep. Below was the river, while on both sides there rose a steep, rocky, and barren gorge. Pete relaxed somewhat, knowing that he had them. They were not going to swim up or down the river; and, even if they had, they would have been slow, easily spotted targets. Any other course they took would have put them up on a steep slope with virtually no cover where rifle with spotlight would make quick work of them.

Pete stopped, readied his rifle, and waited, working the light over the barren ground under some of the sharpest eyes in Africa. They waited and they searched but nothing came up and nothing moved. That left only one possibility. The hyenas had stayed down below the bank on the river's shore.

Pete and his men came over the steep bank, his rifle and their light illuminating the river, both shores and all that lay below. Astonished and perplexed as their eyes scanned, Pete soon lowered his rifle. There were no hyenas, nor any other creatures on four legs. They simply had vanished, as if into the air, with no visible or logical earthly explanation.

There were, however, in the middle of the night in this remote region of the earth, two men at the water's edge. They held strands of hemp adorned with fetishes, which, to those familiar with the African bush, might suggest some things quite obvious given the circumstances. Pete asked them what they were doing.

"Just looking," one of them replied aloofly. He then asked Pete what he was doing. "Looking," he answered quite honestly. The happenings, in our minds at least, surely lend credence to Bror Von Blixen-Finecke's seemingly outrageous hyena story from early 20th-century Kenya.

Be that as it may, the truth, in fact, is more interesting than fiction. Hunting is more interesting and more profitable than any indulgence into fantasy and fiction. And, yes, the witchcraft in Africa is powerful. While the Lord surely works in in mysterious ways, so, too, does the Devil; but we begin to digress.

Reminders of the Creator

Hunting, more than any other endeavor a person can undertake, serves to keep before our eyes and minds the most important eternal and unchanging truth. This is the reason that God finished his dialogue with Job with a reminder of the sheikh's greatest hunting misadventure. Hunting, all the more if done in diverse places amid varieties of wildlife, constantly reminds us of our physical and temporal fragility while, at the same time, granting a quiet, peaceful assurance of a Creator who moves, controls, and sustains with a power and genius we can never fathom. In short, we are continually reminded of the presence, power, and all-seeing eyes of our God. Whether young or old, male or female—such a profound and continual reminder is one from which all may profit.

There, of course, are avid hunters who are atheists—both professed and functional atheists. What must be understood and remembered by all willing honestly to engage in the processes of thought and reason, however, is that atheism is a disease of the heart and soul long before it ever becomes an error of intellect and judgment. All, upon seeing a spectacular presentation of food, a magnificent building, or a fine rifle conclude the presence of a great chef, architect, and gunmaker. Yet some, upon viewing something far more majestic, grand, complex and beautiful—our world and all therein and beyond—deny the possibility of any designing intellect or forming hand. The inconsistency of logic and reason speaks for itself while the testimony of Job 38–41 still stands.

Tests of Character

Finally, hunting teaches the values of good companionship and sound counsel. The presence of both are important in hunting, but in life they are vital. As previously noted, the hunt teaches young people the importance of receiving and heeding good counsel. If not properly taught and guided, then they usually take no game. Having heeded the counsel and lessons that result in their taking of game and in their learning to track, shoot, ride, and to survive in the wild, they will usually then be open to hear and to receive the counsel and lessons on the more important matters of life. The prospect of such an opportunity

Hunting and Life

on behalf of the young is one that should never be forfeited or missed by fathers, grandfathers, uncles, or mentors who have within their resources the means to provide those opportunities.

Whether utilizing a hunt to teach life lessons or engaging solely with peers, the presence of good men and women around you makes the quest both more enjoyable and productive. Conversely, going out into the wild country with one or a few bad people can leave you in regret of the decisions before the first shot is fired or before the first night's fire is kindled. The same will be found to be true in any other endeavor undertaken in life, be it for business or pleasure.

Most interesting, in the matter of determining the good, the bad, and the ugly in people, hunting would seem to possess a uniqueness all its own. The great Roy Rogers once asserted that the best way to get to know a man was to go hunting with him. In our experience, we have found this to be wholly and consistently true. There is no touchstone like the hunt for evaluating and determining character. We have found it to be a reliable test for men and women, young and old. Anyone considering a business partner, a pastor, a mentor for son or daughter, the reliability of a friend or a potential spouse, among other things, should make every effort to take the person in question on a hunt. The more remote and wild the location to be hunted, the better.

The totality of the reason for the reliability of the hunt as a revealer of human character may be open to question, but some lessons can be easily discerned. Most who go out on a hunt wish to take game. Some may become frustrated or angry if they are unable to do so quickly or easily. People may be challenged by harsh terrain or discomforted by heat, cold, rain, or snow. They may be uncomfortable with the proximity of lodging and sleeping and the lack of the amenities of home and city. The constant silence bothers some. Others may be fearful of some of the local critters—bears, poisonous snakes, prowling lions, or nearby hyenas chuckling in the night.

Mysteries of the Bush

When you squeeze a tube of toothpaste, what is inside is fully revealed. Hunting would appear to have a way of squeezing people so as to reveal fully, for good or bad, the truth of what is held but concealed inside. Once far from the lights, noise, and amenities of the city in the silence of the wild country, the human capacity for camouflaging what they would prefer to keep hidden within is stripped away by a convergence of factors.

If a man is selfish, the fact will soon manifest itself. If he has a bad attitude toward people and life in general, then in the proximity of camp, truck, and game trails he will be unable to hide the reality for long. When a man holds perverse or profane thoughts, such will be revealed. If he harbors a bad disposition toward children and young people, and especially if the young are present, the fact will be made manifest, and the children may realize it before the adults do so. When a person does not respond well to hardship or inconvenience, the shortcoming will be clear. A high-maintenance person lacking the virtue of adaptability will stand out clearly. A person harboring a constantly negative disposition will be identified sooner than you may wish.

Yet just as much as hunting squeezes and fully reveals the bad in people, it also presses out and makes manifest the good. A man who shows concern for the wellbeing of an elderly or handicapped hunter or who gives the success of children and youth priority over his own desires reveals his compassion, gentleness, and selflessness. A man who never complains or whines shows resilience, good spirit, and a positive attitude. A man always ready to walk another mile or try something new demonstrates determination, endurance and resourcefulness. If a man relaxes in the silence and is content to let it be, then he is probably a thinker and one who knows the companionship of the mind. If he does not hesitate, confine himself to camp, or always linger in the back in apparent fear, then he likely has courage. His value as a companion in substantive conversation will be realized quickly.

Hunting and Life

Long before getting married, I took my wife hunting and camping several times. From those times together in the wild country of western Texas and northern Mexico, I realized quickly that she was adaptable, resourceful, unafraid, possessed of a sweet spirit and of intellectual curiosity, that she loved children and animals, and that she not only enjoyed the wide open silent places in desert and mountain but craved spending time in them. I learned that she had a game spirit and was open to almost any form of outdoor endeavor and that she was good in conversation regardless of our surroundings. In a revelation that was very important—even crucial to me, I realized quickly that she was not only comfortable and adaptable in the outdoors but that she genuinely liked and respected the animals, wild and domestic, as well as the wonders of the land and resources formed by our Lord's hands. She also took well to a Winchester, thus taken with all else leaving no surprise as to the inevitability of marriage.

To hunt, then, can be regularly to attend the largest, most diverse, and most complete seminary of our God—the one of which He so vividly reminded His servant Job and the only one designed exclusively by His hand. Always we go as a student and sometimes we go as professor as well. There will be times when we are called upon to teach, yet always we learn.

CHAPTER 5

THE HARVEST

Now it came about, when Isaac was old and his eyes were too dim to see, that he called his older son Esau and said to him, "My son." And he said to him, "Here I am." Isaac said, "Behold now, I am old and I do not know the day of my death. Now then, please take your gear, your quiver and your bow, and go out to the field and hunt game for me; and prepare a savory dish for me such as I love, and bring it to me that I may eat, so that my soul may bless you before I die."
GENESIS 27:1-4

As Isaac, the carrier of Abraham's covenant, lay upon his deathbed near the end of his long years, he called for Esau, his firstborn and the stronger of his sons. Interestingly, he requested not the solace of company or strong drink for his stiff and aging body. Rather, he requested that Esau take his quiver and bow and go out into the field and hunt game for him.

In these four verses, Esau is not only portrayed as a mighty and skilled hunter but also as a good cook. Isaac went on to ask that Esau return with the harvested game and prepare for him one of the savory dishes that he loved. The request is made more interesting by the fact that Isaac had his own herds. He had plenty of sheep, goats, and perhaps some cattle as well. He could have requested the preparation of a prime lamb, young goat, or maybe some beef tenderloin, which many today, especially with regard to the lamb and beef, would consider to be tastier fare. Yet Isaac specifically requested wild game prepared with his firstborn son's culinary expertise. So seriously did the dying patriarch take the request that he ended it with the phrase, ". . . so that my soul may bless you before I die."

Though not surprising, the fact that in Isaac's dependency and fragility, he called upon his strongest and boldest son is significant. When people are helpless, hurt, in need, or feel endangered, they want men of strength, skills, and courage at their side—an age-old truth. Machismo and the praise of the virtues of valor, strength, and martial prowess may have fallen out of fashion amid the onslaught of political correctness and glorification of effete, self-centered males. Yet still when endangered, people call for the police. Trapped by raging fire, they call for highly trained firefighters with the courage to run into the very flames that everyone else is running away from. Some among the leftist students rescued by the United States Marines amid the chaos of Grenada in 1983 admitted afterward that they had never been so happy to see soldiers. Our sharp-shooting, devil-dog life-takers and heartbreakers along with combined U.S. Army and Navy forces suddenly became beautiful in the limited vision and minds of the students—our words, not theirs, as ours more wholly capture the facts here.

Being weak and utterly helpless, Isaac called upon his strong son, Esau. His second son Jacob, though Esau's twin, was timid and less aggressive. Jacob would be described today as a "mama's boy." In our era he would have felt more at home at the mall or the Internet café than in the field. In his own time he was more adept at helping his mother with chores around the home and hearth, a fact of which Isaac was well aware.

The Harvest

The covenant between God and Abraham, nevertheless, was destined to pass through Jacob rather than Esau. For it has always been a propensity of our God, in demonstrating His absolute power and sovereignty, sometimes to work through the least rather than the great in carrying out His plan. So it was here, though Jacob, to his credit, did toughen up in the end. After an all-night wrestling match with God on the banks of the Jabbok River, in which the patriarch came away with a lifelong limp from a dislocated thigh socket, Jacob earned both his blessing from the Lord and his new name, Israel, meaning "strives with God."

Savory Meat

Isaac, though, more than any other earthly desire, wished to savor some of Esau's game at least once more. Most who have partaken of properly cared for and well-prepared venison will need no explanation here. No red meat is leaner, more nutritious, or, when passed from a skilled hunter to the hands of an adept cook, any more savory. The game that Isaac so desired could have been roebuck, ibex, or Arabian onyx. Our best guess is that the tenderloins or backstraps of the gazelle were foremost on his mind. Mountain gazelles were common in the region and, in our experience, make for delicious steaks or shish kebobs, among other dishes. Whatever game Esau harvested, it was Isaac's intention to take in all that he could hold, savoring every bite, and then to impart a blessing unto Esau in return for the blessing of the game.

Insofar as the protein requisite to human health, strength, and survival, the abundance and variety of wild game and fish is foremost among the blessings of our Lord. Blessed in its life-sustaining virtues, it imparts equal blessing in the versatility and savory variety in which the meat may be prepared and enjoyed. That so many people seem to have been soured to the culinary prospects of game by an unfavorable first experience, while perhaps sometimes due to a predetermined set of mind, generally stems from failure to dress, clean, prepare, package, or season and cook the meat properly. Quite often the failure involves some combination of the above if not all.

For the hunt to be properly executed and complete, much more comes into account than simply getting a bullet, arrow, or spear into the right part of an animal. Just as the hunt can never attain the fullness of its potential or purpose apart from the teaching of the spiritual and temporal lessons of life to the young, neither can the experiences be complete in absence of the process of teaching the proper care and preparation of the meat. First of all, to leave good, life-sustaining meat in the field or to throw it away because of neglect, in our view, is an affront to the God who has provided it and given us the privilege of taking it. Second, to serve game not properly prepared or cooked—and hence not savory—to family, friends, and guests is to shortchange both you and all at your table. After all, had Esau not been willing and able to complete his hunts by preparing the harvest of the field and bringing it to the table in a variety of tasty creations, there would have been neither the craving nor the request of his father Isaac.

Thanks and Giving

The harvest of the field should never be taken for granted and must always be honored. Once an animal has been taken, we commonly kneel and lift up a brief prayer of thanksgiving to our Lord who has provided both the game and the opportunity to hunt. Honor and gratitude, though, will always be best demonstrated by the attitude carried and the way that the meat of blessing is cared for, distributed, and utilized.

We have often distributed significant portions of our harvests, once the meat has been prepared and packaged, to the poor, the sick, and to those who love wild game but lack either the opportunity or the health to go afield themselves. Many other hunters do the same. To do so regularly is one of the methods by which boys and young men can be taught the importance of being providers, of demonstrating compassion and generosity, and to put the needs and well-being of others before their own inclinations and desires.

To have provided others in need with savory, life-sustaining food taken by his hand, and with his strength, work, savvy, and skills will usually leave the boy or young man with a visceral understanding of the concepts of compassion and provision and also with a level of satisfaction that is unlikely to be equaled by any other forms of teaching. To go to the store and buy food for someone in need, while perfectly honorable and good, is yet as different as the night from the day in such a way that the two distinct acts will be felt and will resonate in the minds and hearts of the young. They will always be more proud of, and take greater satisfaction in, the gift that first was procured and processed by their own newly acquired masculine prowess and skills and then given. Most important, though, they are learning the biblical obligation, as well as the joy, of providing for, giving to, and caring for others. More simply put, they are learning the actions of love and the ways of our Lord. Neither the giving nor the personal enjoyment of the meat of the harvest can be accomplished without the knowledge of how to take the game properly from the field to the table.

More Than "Droppin' the Hammer"

"There's a lot more to deer huntin' than just droppin' the hammer on one." These words, though spoken to me some thirty-four years ago, have remained always as clear in my mind as if uttered the day before. They came from Jerry, the west Texas rancher who was to become my father "west of the Pecos." Tired and cold, deep into a frigid, late December night at the end of my first, long, hands-on lesson in the proper and meticulous processing of multiple deer, I had made a comment about the amount of work and time involved. Jerry's laconic, understated maxim was given in reply.

In fact, one of the most important lessons to be taught to young men is that virtually the whole animal has significant value. When Armour was nine, he was thrilled to take a beautiful rattlesnake in far west Texas. As he admired his snake from a safe distance, Jerry Davenport said, "Beautiful snake. Skin it." "Touch it?" responded Armour. "Don't rightly know how you can skin it without touching it," reflected the rancher. Removing the head first, Armour skinned the snake, which made him a beautiful belt that he wore for some years. And that was easier than the porcupine! But quill lamps are gorgeous even when you do not have a hankering for more than one. Lesson learned. All animals are God's creation and are valuable to man. One does not just go out and begin shooting. Every "trophy" is carefully preserved.

Indeed, there is so much more to the hunt, in many respects, than merely "dropping the hammer" on a steady, well-aimed Winchester. Yet for all the long hours spent processing and packaging year upon year, for us—those within our circle—and many who have crossed our paths, the manifold blessings of lean, savory protein accompanied by good fellowship through the entirety of the year ahead have proven a cherished and more than ample reward for the work done. Further, there is a level of satisfaction and appreciation for food—whether grown or harvested with rifle, shotgun, bow, or other weaponry and taken by your own work, savvy, and skill—which can never be equaled by returns from the local supermarket.

Superior Sustenance

Facts, however, are neither the only nor the best reason for taking as much of your protein as possible from the varied bounty of wild game. There simply is no way to describe the American meat and dairy industries other than to note that they are largely polluted with much that should never enter the human body. There are now more healthy

Paige Patterson in the Zambian Bush.

Paige with Rachel and Armour and Armour's Eland.

Children in Zambian orphanage.

Armour in African Bush.

Paige Patterson's Lioness Trophy in the President's Office at SWBTS.

Paige with PH and tracking team for lioness.

Paige with hippo taken in Zimbabwe.

Paige walking lions with Andy Connally in Zimbabwe.

Herd of young eland.

Camp in the African Bush.

Paige with crocodile taken in South Africa.

Father and Sons – Armour, Dad, Mark

Armour and Dad and Rachel with her zebra taken in Zambia.

The Howell family – Carmen, Mark, Rebekah and Abigail – with record Red Hartebeest taken by Mark.

alternatives than ever before in modern times—organic meat and dairy without antibiotics, added hormones, steroids, and from animals not fed animal byproducts. That such products, at much higher prices, have sold well is testimony to a significant number of people who have realized or at least suspected that much of what is being purveyed is unhealthy and possibly dangerous. If you have done no more than just to observe the major headlines over the past couple of decades, then you know that what is being fed and otherwise put into the animals that end up packed in our grocery stores, along with the products they render, is suspect at best.

Furthermore, the vast array of junk food consumed by most people from the contents of a bag or box is loaded with ingredients that clearly are unhealthy at best and, in the case of some, surely harmful. All who care about their own nutrition and health, as well as that of their children, should avoid the majority of all processed foods. A standard rule of thumb is that, if it comes in a bag or box, be wary of it. Be wary even of processed foods touting the absence of MSG, as you should know that there are multiple other substances—more than ten—containing MSG that can legally be used and listed, with no denotation being given of the actual presence of MSG.

Processed Soy

The worst additive among American dietary staples, and one that with time and the accumulation of deleterious effects may well be revealed as such, is a relatively modern one. The United States is now, by far, the world's leading producer of soybeans—even more than China and Japan. The reasons that this has come to be would require a chapter, if not a book. Suffice it here to note that, in a nutshell, it all comes down to money. As in other matters, those who already have a lot of money have figured out how to make even more through the economic boon of the soybean. Soybeans are cheap, easy to grow in many regions, and come with numerous agricultural and economic advantages for farmers.

Processed soy in multiple forms is a product, which, because of its being cheap and thus surety to swell profit margins, is being forced down American throats in unprecedented variety and volume. Any inclined to be skeptical should start reading labels on all products they buy. Processed soy, usually in the form of soybean oil but also in other products such as soy protein or soy lecithin, is in almost everything. Desserts, salad dressings, chocolate, snack foods, pasta sauces, bread of all kinds (try finding hamburger buns without soybean oil) and especially the sandwich bread and rolls and loaves that are sold in conventional grocery stores, canned fish, canned and boxed soups—the list is endless.

Those arguing that all soy is healthy due to the fact that women in some Asian countries have lower rates of breast cancer—and other kinds of cancer as well—than women in the United States and other developed countries are operating with a false premise. Having traveled extensively in Asia, we have yet to find a single country or culture that cooks with or otherwise utilizes soybean oil. They do ingest a substantial amount of soybeans, but most of that appears to come from fermented soy. Soy sauce, when properly brewed in the traditional way, is fermented. Miso, likewise, is fermented. Fermented soy has been shown not to have the estrogen-spiking effect of processed soy.

The unprecedented American utilization of processed soy is not a derivation of traditional Asian culinary arts. The American use of the soybean is something wholly new, untested, and thus devoid of any verifiable track record. To do the best for yourself and your family with regard to food, nutrition, and health, you would seem wise to avoid anything new and untested. That would be anything without a track record to verify long-term results.

The Harvest

Soybean Oil

Those who are skeptical should also start to inquire as to the kind of oil used in restaurants they frequent. Most American restaurants have become standing, active monuments to soybean oil. Virtually all fast food and chain restaurants use soybean oil primarily or solely. When asked, they will often reply that they use pure vegetable oil—and indeed, it is the words "vegetable oil" that usually appear in big black letters on the front of the plastic jug. The tiny letters on the back of the jug, however, in accordance with the requirements of the law in revealing contents, will almost always reveal pure soybean oil. On some there will be a mix of soybean with other cheap oils.

Now, when considering the wholesome vegetables most commonly recommended by nutritionists and other health experts, likely you will think of broccoli, cauliflower, Brussels sprouts, kale, and other leafy greens. Yet we have never found the oils of any of these most nutritious vegetables in vegetable oil. Why, then, is soybean oil so often marketed as vegetable oil? The reasons are twofold. First and most common, food producers and restaurateurs are attempting to disguise the fact that they are selling you a product as inferior and cheap as their money can buy so as to glean the greatest profit they can from your investment. An example of this is the olive oil mayonnaise put out by one major producer. The words "olive oil" appear in large green letters on the front of the jar, but the same words in tiny black letters on the back under the list of ingredients come only after—denoting less in quantity—the tiny black letters spelling out "soybean oil." The disguise should not be difficult to see through. The denotation of "vegetable," in the eyes of a consumer, will always seem more healthful and to be of greater substance than that of "processed soybean."

The second reason for the use of the deceptive and inaccurate label of "vegetable oil," unfortunately, is probably more nefarious and morally unjustifiable. While most restaurateurs, store owners, and the like may not realize the deleterious effects of the product, there are surely some in the upper echelons of production and business who either suspect or know the dangers posed and damage done; and, therefore, they try to distance the product as much as is possible under law from the reality of what it is. Considering the knowledge and scientific findings now available, coupled with the clear efforts at deception and disguise, it becomes difficult to arrive objectively at any other conclusion.

An oncologist with whom my wife Rachel and I talked a few years ago, while telling her ways to give herself as much protection as possible from breast cancer, warned us to avoid all processed soy. Having referenced the vast and tragic sweep of breast cancer throughout women of all ages across our nation, he then added that he was also treating an inordinate number of male breast cancer cases. When I asked him his opinion of why this was occurring, he said that "for one thing, our whole population is swimming in soybean oil." Soybean oil, and all processed soy, he went on to explain, mimics estrogen and thus causes estrogen levels in the body—for men and women—to rise. Elevated estrogen, we now know, is conclusively linked to breast cancer.

Naturally Better Track Records

Olive oil, butter, and ghee (clarified butter) have a track record millennia long. Sesame oil, peanut oil, and coconut oil have a track record. Wheat, barley, millet, quinoa, rice, and yoghurt (in its whole and plain forms) can be traced back through the ages. Wild game of all kinds—organic, free-roaming, lean, and non-GMO—has a track record that has remained the same from the ancient days of Nimrod up until today. Thus we have a befuddling irony that so many in the crowd who champion the production, imbibing, and eating of all things organic and non-GMO then lead the calls for an end to hunting. For nothing is more organic, non-GMO, and free-roaming than the meat of the wildlife that roam upon and draw sustenance from the wild places of the earth.

The Harvest

We cannot know or be aware of all things and cannot keep all that is harmful out of our bodies. As stated previously, living is the single most dangerous thing you can do. These facts, however, in no way constitute reason or justification for doing nothing. Consider what good may be accomplished, and what harm might be avoided, if we act decisively and aggressively upon what we can and do know.

Intentionally Better Choices

We seldom eat out, as we refuse to let anyone or any entity determine what we or our families will and will not eat. We refuse to pay the same and rising prices for the cheapest of ingredients. When we do eat out, we do so selectively and aggressively, avoiding most offerings and inquiring specifically as to what ingredients are used in any dish we might order. Some of this information can now be found also on restaurant web sites.

When we go to grocery stores, we shop offensively and aggressively, meaning that we read the fine print on the labels of everything we might purchase every time we take anything off the shelf. This method is the only safe response to this threat—constant vigilance—by which you can consistently avoid the polluted junk that producers and retailers want to force down your throat. Such will mean an end to some favorite snacks and sweets. Likely it will mean that you begin to make more things at home from scratch with whole ingredients. You may be inclined to start baking your own bread. The sum of it all entails more effort, work, and awareness on your part, but in accordance with the ways of the world and the nature of man, it is the only way by which quality nourishment and sound health for you and your family have the best chance of being sustained.

Hunting, for us, is a component of the commitment and resolve to put the best and most wholesome food upon our tables. As is evident, hunting cannot be the only facet of such a commitment. How and where you shop, how you eat when on the road, where and what you eat in restaurants, and certain aspects of lifestyle (active versus sedentary, for example) must also be considered.

Whether you hunt extensively or just on occasion, any wild game put into your freezer is a valuable contribution to nutrition and health. Whether utilized as a staple or a supplement, organic wild meat is as wholesome and nourishing a food—and surpassing all other forms of protein—as can be put into the body. In addition to the health and nutritive superiority of wild game, wildlife puts notably less pressure on the land than does livestock simply because wild animals were designed and made for the land upon which they indigenously live just as the land was designed and made for them. Further, wildlife, when properly managed through an intelligent program of sustained yield, is an easily renewable resource.

The Blessing of Wild Game

Our love and gratitude for the women, boys, girls, young women, and young men in our lives is such that we refuse knowingly to put estrogen or any other harmful substance into their bodies. The blessing of the meat of wild game—be it venison, javelina, wild boar, bear, feral hog, duck, quail, dove, antelope, or any other—is too precious, not to mention delicious, to be polluted with deleterious garbage like soybean oil or MSG. The physical blessing and benefit it imparts to the body is too great to be mixed with and countered by any intake of inferior and damaging ingredients or processed foods. The game of the wild lands, our lives, our bodies, and our health are all gifts of our God. Each should be treated as such with gratitude and with all due diligence.

A benefit of the properly executed hunt linked to the blessing of the organic meat is that boys and young men learn the process and skills of taking food from the field to the plate. Though viewed by many as obsolete skills, it is our view, nonetheless, that the skills and process should be learned by all young men and by young women who demonstrate interest. You can never know when such skills may be called upon.

Even the illustrious and intelligent Mrs. Patterson, or Mama Armour, as the Africans called her (following their custom of listing the name of the oldest son linked to the term of endearment), eventually found herself in an unexpected dilemma. She had spent years shunning the sight, taste, and touch of the meat of any game. After our first successful harvest in Tanzania, we, our tracker, two missionaries, and their wives set about the long process of butchering the game and cutting and packing the meat. Mrs. Patterson quickly realized how inappropriate and wrong it would appear if she, being consistent with her lifelong vow, was the only one to refuse to lend a hand in the preparation of the meat to be distributed among the missionaries and the local seminary students and their families. To her credit, she put aside her inhibitions and stood up to the challenge. After receiving a quick crash course in the cutting and packing of game, she grabbed a knife and some freezer paper and gave it her best.

Survival Skills

Another reward of the harvest when the hunt, in all facets, is fully engaged, is that the young can attain a full understanding of the food chain, the ecosystems upon which it depends, and their place within them. Remember that the intellectual knowledge of particular facts versus an actual experience-based, inherent understanding of them can be two very different things and are not always manifested as a pair. Most people eat meat, fowl, seafood, or some combination thereof, but few have much substantial knowledge with regard to land and ecosystems. Few have seen the animal whose meat they chew when that animal was alive a few hours or days before they commenced to eating.

Mysteries of the Bush

This is true because most do not hunt. Fewer still have truly worked the land and taken their living from it. Few have truly engaged wild country on its terms. Even when visiting national parks, game reserves or other remote areas, most are never far from the comfortable resorts in which they will spend a warm or air-conditioned night.

Most have never carried the meat to be consumed in the coming months over long distances. They have not carried or dragged a deer for several miles in rugged terrain. They have not quartered and packed an elk out of the high country or tracked an animal for winding miles in harsh elements just to try to get off a clear shot.

Food taken in harsh conditions—that is, worked for and even struggled for—begets a gratitude and an appreciation not possible in return from a successful shopping venture at the local supermarket. Hunting affords the preeminent opportunity to teach the young such appreciation and gratitude for the bounty and blessings provided by our Lord. Too, there is little that can make a young man more proud or gain more confidence than to eat, and to see others enjoy, the meat that he brought to the table via his own rifle or bow and skills of preparation.

Every young man should have the confidence that, wherever there are critters, he can provide a meal if he needs to—even if he has to take it first from field or pasture. Survival situations still can and do occur, and they can be brought about by various factors for many different reasons. Furthermore, in depressed and uncertain economic times, it is not wise to presume anything or to take times of security and plenty for granted. There is much within our system and society that is more fragile than may be realized. We cannot know what will come. Young men should be trained and ready for as many potential situations and challenges as is possible. They should know how to find and provide all the basic necessities in the case of emergencies or challenging times; shelter, warmth, clean water, fire, and food. Hunting teaches lessons with regard to all.

You do not buy insurance because you hope to use it. You do not train to fight because you desire combat. You acquire insurance and build combat skills with the hope that you never have to use them. The same is true of survival skills learned in hunting, which many deem to be obsolete. You will want to use some of them but would prefer that it not have to be in a desperate fight to survive. Simply put, it is wise to hope and pray for the best while always being prepared for the worst. Teaching young men how to live off of the land is a significant part of that preparation.

Science Lessons

Within that process, the young also learn about the land, the animals they hunt, and the other wild critters that, in many regions, will also cross their paths amid the pursuit. They learn the foods that the animals depend upon, their sources of water, where they seek cover, and where they sleep. They will learn how the animals mate and care for their young. In ranching areas, they will learn which kinds of livestock, based upon what and how they eat, complement the feeding patterns of wildlife and which kinds compete more directly with them—an important aspect of understanding with regard to conservation.

Hunters as Conservationists

None are more ardent conservationists than are hunters who have been properly taught and trained. For one thing, they desire that there always be game to hunt. Thus they, more than any others, realize the importance of not overhunting a species and not allowing land to be overgrazed. Having observed the animals closely upon their terms, their observations encompassing many more and varied animals than they ever will shoot, and having seen what they eat, where they drink, and where they hide, hunters hold perspective and understanding unavailable to the suburban-dwelling, anti-hunting crowd who walk the streets yelling and carrying signs of protest. The suburbanites may have a fond memory or two of approaching bison or a moose in Yellowstone with fifty other tourists also crowded about taking photographs. Such "adventures" pale before the intimacy and raw authenticity of a hunter's experience. Animals in national parks or reserves, being accustomed to the constant presence and flow of humans with cameras, behave and react much differently than do critters in regions still truly and wholly wild. They still are wild and will attack the vulnerable and naïve tourist or backpacker—which does happen with amusing regularity—but their behavior and patterns are not the same.

In all of my time in the truly wild country of east and southern Africa, I have actually seen a leopard on only three occasions that come to mind. Twice the sightings were fleeting, just a glimpse for a second or two and the big cat was gone. Such are the norm in leopard encounters, for their senses are all extremely sharp, they are very fast, and God has given them the perfect camouflage for the country they inhabit. They are solitary cats that prefer to see and not be seen and are quite adept in so doing. Yet there are certain parks and reserves in Africa where almost every tourist "spots" a leopard, and often one with a fresh "kill." Go and figure how such staging is done!

Hunters not only better understand animal behavior and patterns, but also will have much greater understanding, and thus a greater appreciation of the remarkable capacities and keenness of senses possessed by them. They will have seen—and sometimes felt—demonstrations of their speed and strength. They will know how difficult it can be to get close to them, or even to achieve a distant glimpse, when the animals do not want to be approached or seen.

The sum of the hunter's experience and learning culminate in the élan of a true conservationist. From a fullness of understanding of the animals, the land they inhabit, and man's vital relationship to both comes the spirit, soul, and mind of genuine conservation. The majesty of beast and sustenance of earth are ascertained in equal measure with the requisite role and obligation of man.

Therein is to be found the core of the genuine conservational spirit innate to the hunter's soul. When we consider the manifold provisions of the land for both man and beast and realize our utter dependence upon them, a spirit of humility and gratitude becomes the only option to an open mind. When we contemplate the beasts of the field and birds of the air and consider the attributes that we so admire—their strength, speed, beauty and majesty—we can only conclude that the God who designed them and gave them life also cherishes and admires the same. In addition, we cannot observe the remarkable variety of creatures and their diverse patterns of living and not also see a God of imaginative genius who also loves diversity. As much as we see His love of beauty and majesty, we also see in certain critters put forth by His hand irrefutable evidence of a divine sense of humor.

To behold a God who loves and values these same things that we so cherish and then to stand in His presence amid His glory leaves upon us the obligation to protect and to sustain the beloved work and gift of His hands. We must protect and preserve this creation so cherished by Him. Because He clearly and inherently loves and admires such attributes and beauty, we, too, must be possessed of a genuine appreciation of the same. In fact, any who fail to be awed and profoundly moved by the attributes of the creatures and the wonders of the land in which they dwell have then failed both in understanding and in a facet of their obligations and relationship to their Creator and Lord.

Most hunters have no difficulty with such concepts, having experienced intimately the power, majesty, diversity, and beauty that abounds. They remain very much aware of how small and temporally insignificant they are in standing in the presence of it all. None, more than they, so admires and cherishes the beasts of the field. None respects and values the land upon which we and all creatures depend any more.

Hunters' Respect for the Animals

We can dispense with the ludicrous and indefensible allegation, from the anti-hunting crowd and from others, that the killing of an animal precludes any possibility of respect and love for the same. These generally angry individuals and groups emanating from the stillborn soul of the godless secular left are the same ones who so often extol the pure and untarnished virtue of all people and things Native American. We, too, admire Native Americans, though our reasons for so doing are rooted in reality and not in the imaginings and fantasies of the secular left.

The Native Americans of the Great Plains hunted the herds of bison constantly. They hunted and took other animals as well. Hunting was an inseparable component of the culture. Yet they did not in any way hate or disrespect the animals that they hunted and killed. To the contrary, all evidence verifies beyond shadow of doubt that they not only respected the bison but, in fact, admired and revered them. They realized how dependent they were upon that one animal and understood the fullness of its provisions. From the bison came their food, clothing, lodging, and blankets. They revered the bison not only for what it provided but also for its strength and spirit. Further, they recognized that some power bigger and greater than they had given both the bison and the land to them.

To love, respect, and even to revere the animal that you hunt is not only possible but also is common. Among men and women who hunt, respect and reverence for the animals hunted is a mindset so prevalent as to constitute the prevailing rule. To understand wholly the magnitude of all that has been given us in the creatures put forth by our God in the wild and largely uninhabited regions of the earth is a reward of the hunt that becomes the parturition of perspective, gratitude, respect, and honor.

The Harvest

Protection of Wildlife's Value

There is a sad yet very real and immutable fact of which hunters would seem to be much more keenly aware than the majority of those who do not hunt. In order for wildlife to survive in significant numbers and for their habitats to remain protected, in any region or country, they must retain monetary value and impart economic benefit. In moral terms, this is not the way that it should be. Nevertheless, it is and will remain the absolute reality. Of the funds utilized to protect and preserve wildlife and habitat on any continent, no individuals—tourists or recreationists or any sort—contribute as much of their hard-earned cash as do hunters. In North America, South America, Africa, Asia, Australia, and the Pacific Islands, hunters pay sums far in excess of those necessitated by the more common endeavors of other travelers in like regions.

For example, in southern Africa you can spend two or three nights in a plush resort in a national park and go out on a "camera safari" and see cape buffalo, lions, and elephants while, for that period of time and activity, spending less than $1,000. To hunt and shoot a cape buffalo in the same region, you will pay $15,000 or more just for the buffalo alone, not to include the services of a professional hunter, lodging, and food. To shoot a lion or an elephant, you will pay anywhere from $20,000 to $30,000 or more.

Closer to home, in Arizona you can drive around or hike, viewing and photographing all the elk you may desire for just the cost of the gas in your vehicle. If an easy and up-close encounter is desired, then you can just pay the $25 to enter Grand Canyon National Park. If, on the other hand, you wish to hunt elk in Arizona, you will pay a minimum of around $300 just for license and tag. Depending upon where you are from and in which part of the state you wish to hunt, the sum could be closer to $1,000 and the hunt itself can rise in cost to well over $20,000. Hunters, then, because they cherish their time and experiences among

135

the most majestic creatures in the wild, pristine lands that remain and treasure the physical and spiritual sustenance gained thereby, and because they desire that their children and grandchildren be able to experience the same, pay the heaviest price for the preservation and protection of both animals and land.

The hunt is incomplete apart from the sustenance of the harvest. Likewise, the physical facets of the hunt, when such are all that is sought and taken, remain insufficient. For the blessings and rewards of the hunt to be fully experienced, carried, and then passed down, the spiritual must be sought, discovered, and embraced just as the physical. What is majestic but temporal must be appreciated and taken within the vision of that which holds supreme and eternal. While the creatures of the land are to be admired, respected, and revered, and then preserved for coming generations, the Lord remains the One who gave the breath of life to all and is thus to be remembered, revered, and honored above all.

CHAPTER 6

THE SPIRIT, THE SOUL, AND THE SILENT PLACES

My soul waits in silence for God only;
From Him is my salvation.
Psalm 62:1

The Lord is good to those who wait for Him,
To the person who seeks Him.
It is good that he waits silently
For the salvation of the Lord.
It is good for a man that he should bear
The yoke in his youth.
Let him sit alone and be silent
Since He has laid *it* on him.
Let him put his mouth in the dust,
Perhaps there is hope.

Lamentations 3:25-29

"But there are no words that can tell the hidden spirit of the wilderness, that can reveal its mystery, its melancholy and its charm. There is delight in the hardy life of the open, in long rides rifle in hand, in the thrill of the fight with dangerous game. Apart from this, yet mingled with it, is the strong attraction of the silent places...."

So wrote the avid hunter, warrior, statesman, and American president Theodore Roosevelt about the inscrutable spirit of the wild and the solace of the silent places. Indeed, there are no words by which to do justice and capture that hidden yet palpable and impelling presence felt and known intimately to all who have carried their rifles into the wildest and most remote of the silent realms. Knowing we will fall short, still we try.

The extent to which Teddy Roosevelt endorsed this idea is nowhere clearer than in the chilling book *The River of Doubt.* Here his near-death experience of being the first non-Indian to traverse the Amazon jungle's River of Doubt just because it had never been done. Food was everywhere, but remained inaccessible to the party. Many died of injury, disease, hunger, or poison darts. Miraculously, Teddy survived, more proud of this exploit than of his presidency of the United States.

What draws men, old and young, to fill their minds and pull irresistibly upon the deepest, hidden realms of spirit and soul? What does the same within many women, drawing them away from the comfort and ease of the company and activities of their peers toward places and endeavors long presumed not to be the realm of the fairer sex? What is this implacable force?

The hunt is about much more than the taking of game, imparting the most profound ramifications and profluent rewards. Moreover, to hunt is to seek far more than to feed and nourish the body with the prime meat of the blessed harvest. At the core of the quest, venture afield and hunt in the wild, silent places is to feed the ever-yearning human spirit and soul with the sustenance found in full in only one place.

That place may be in North America, South America, Africa, Asia, Europe, the frozen far north, or the Pacific islands. The topography,

The Spirit, the Soul, and the Silent Places

climate, and terrain of the locales differ, as do the wild creatures inhabiting them, but the place—and the spirit-renewing, soul-fortifying nourishment it silently yields—is the same. The place and the vital nourishment imparted remain the same, as do the appetite and need in a man's spirit and soul.

As the highest percentage of our population in history now dwells within the crowded, noise-ridden urban and suburban centers, and with the relentless press and expansion of the role of technology in all of our lives, the need for the vital sustenance of the silent places is likely greater than it has ever been, regardless of the state of the appetite. The youth or young professional, for example, who assures you that he needs no more for contentment and fulfillment in life than his smartphone, television, skateboard, latte bar, night clubs, and trips to the mall obviously possesses neither the knowledge, vision, nor wisdom to understand that he surely and desperately needs much more. His dereliction of mind, effeteness of spirit, and destitution of soul are conditions of which he is wholly unaware.

Experiencing the Wilderness

Abraham, Job, Moses, David, Elijah, Elisha, Amos, Jesus, and Paul—among other great men of the Bible—all spent significant time in the desert and/or in other realms of wilderness. All knew intimately the draw and attraction of the hidden spirit of the wild, silent places. Their spirits and souls had partaken of, and been fortified by, the sacred sustenance to be found only therein.

Humans need the fellowship and companionship of other humans. Such are needs innate in our creation. We need the spiritual gatherings of the congregation of believers. As there is an appointed time for every event under heaven, we need the festivities of the social gatherings of families, friends, and acquaintances. We need to play, sing, dine together, and converse. Yet just as much as we need all of these things, and in certain times and situations even more than we need them, the human spirit, soul, mind, and body need the solace, solitude, stillness, quiet, purity, mystery, beauty, vastness, and majesty of the silent places. At times they require even the hardship, the challenge, and the danger inherent in varying measure in the remotest of the wild realms. Young men, particularly, need to be challenged, and they should endeavor to challenge themselves. To paraphrase Lamentations, it is good for them to bear the yoke of the silent places, and that they taste the dust of the ground (Lamentations 3:27-28).

To bear the yoke of the burden of the hardship and work generally inherent to any venture into wild country builds the strength that is the glory of young men. To have to push themselves to overcome challenges builds confidence, perseverance, resourcefulness, and innovational creativity. To face danger, standing firm in its face, builds courage and grants perspective, both of which are conspicuously and increasingly absent in our postmodern culture—the latter perhaps even more so than the former. To taste the dust reminds us from whence we came and of that to which our bodies return. More important, we are reminded of the ground upon which all of us utterly depend, regardless of where we live, and that sustains both man and beast. The subtle crunch and taste of dust in a dry mouth generally inclines an individual to speak less—a valuable lesson to teach the young.

The Emptiness of Wordiness

Many within our society and culture speak far too often and, in so doing, remarkably manage to reveal an ironic sum, which at once constitutes disturbingly too much and distressingly too little. The sum is too much merely for the sheer volume of words, the incessancy with which they flow, and the crassness and frivolity of what is laid bare and in full before the public. The sum is too little for the lack of meaningful substance, knowledge, or wisdom to be found in the words.

The Spirit, the Soul, and the Silent Places

Ecclesiastes 5:7 declares that "in many words there is emptiness." The voice of a fool comes through many words, and thus our words should be few (Ecclesiastes 5:2-3). Proverbs 10:19 warns, "When there are many words, transgression is unavoidable, but he who restrains his lips is wise." Proverbs 17:27 states, "He who restrains his words has knowledge," and the following verse goes further, noting that, "Even a fool, when he keeps silent, is considered wise."

There clearly can be no biblical justification of, or allowance for, many words and incessant chatter. In addition to the consequences stated in Proverbs 10:19 and Ecclesiastes 5:7, the primary reason for this is that, when you speak, you are not listening, hearing (there can be a difference), observing or learning. Too, apparently—sometimes painfully so—most who are talking constantly are doing so apart from the exercise and burden of thought.

Many of us, on at least a few occasions, have tried to give counsel to a person who simply would not close his mouth. Most have attempted conversation with such an individual. The words never cease and may be accompanied by perpetual texting or the ever-present noise of music or television, which they refuse to shut off. If you have encountered such individuals, then try to recall your inner feelings and reactions and your ultimate course of action. We can tell you frankly what ours always has been and will continue to be. We quickly become irritated and disgusted by such behavior. Except for the cases when the individual involved is a young person whom we have been called to mentor, we simply shut down and then politely remove ourselves from the person's presence at the first opportunity. Your reactions were likely similar. Why, then, should we expect the reaction of our God, the giver of life and of every gift we enjoy therein to have impulses and reactions much different than our own in the face of such behavior? Indeed, a preponderance of Scripture suggests that He might have even less tolerance for the frivolities, noise, and many words of a fool than do many of us.

Silence and Stillness

The practice of silence contributes significantly to the overall health of body and mind. The number of Americans and Europeans who now practice some form of meditation—many going to studios, gyms, temples, or retreats specifically designed for such—bears testimony to some level of understanding of the fact among a small segment of society. As beneficial as the practice of silence is to the body and mind, though, the practice becomes not only one of benefit but one also essential and vital to the health and fortification of the spirit and soul. Furthermore, the seeking of our God, the meaningful pursuit of His ways, and the discernment of His will and guiding hand through the feel or sound of His still, small voice in conjunction with knowledge of self and accurate interpretation of circumstances and formative events cannot commence apart from a commitment to the practice of silence.

Thus David wrote often of silence and stillness while pursuing, yet waiting, upon the Lord. "My soul *waits* in silence for God only; from Him is my salvation" (Psalm 62:1). Jeremiah emphasized the importance of silence in Lamentations: "The LORD is good to those who wait for Him, to the person who seeks Him. *It is* good that he waits silently . . . Let him sit alone and be silent . . ." (Lamentations 3:25-26, 28).

We cannot come to God—receiving Him, His blessings, or the guiding of His words and hand—in the manner of our own choosing. All must come to God on His terms, and upon His terms only. Nowhere is the table so perfectly or beautifully set for the confluence of the soul of man with the presence and voice of the Lord than in the solitude of the silent places in the wild.

The Spirit, the Soul, and the Silent Places

"You prepare a table before me in the presence of my enemies; You have anointed my head with oil; My cup overflows," David wrote as he reflected upon his quiet fellowship with the Lord in the wild, silent, and ever-dangerous Judean hills.

To hunt in the lonely, silent places does not guarantee any interaction with, or blessing from, the Lord. What is assured, rather, is an opportunity to reach out to our Lord on His terms, from His seminary and sanctuary, and to receive His presence, His comfort, His peace, His counsel, and the touch of His guiding staff. Free of the noise, distractions, bustle, and obligations of inhabited lands, and still unmarred by hands of men, in the silent places are set and established the terms of our Lord more wholly, perfectly, and beautifully than can be encountered in any other place. The stage for communion with Him is set as it can be nowhere else.

The practice of silence, however, necessitates an adeptness in the art of stillness. Baroness Karen Blixen, who penned the stirring, beautiful book *Out of Africa*,[6] once observed that civilized man had lost the aptitude for stillness.[7] She made an acute observation.

To practice silence, you must first possess the aptitude for stillness. Most expcrienced hunters have learned the art of stillness, especially those who have hunted with bow or spear. Thus they, upon entry into the silent places, are better established than most to encounter the presence of the Lord.

David wrote of stillness in Psalm 4:4: "Meditate in your heart upon your bed, and be still." The sons of Korah emphasized the importance of stillness in Psalm 46:10: "Cease striving and know that I am God," or

---

[6] The book was published under Blixen's more familiar pen name, Isak Dinesen.

[7] Karen Blixen, *Out of Africa*, Penguin Essentials (New York: Random House, 1937, 1938), 16.

as rendered in the King James Version more familiar to most, "Be still, and know that I am God."

Stillness and silence are not necessary in attaining the salvation of Jesus Christ, and for a great multitude of modern souls, this is a fortunate thing. However, the active coupling of stillness and silence remains imperative for spiritual growth, the building of knowledge, and the acquisitions of wisdom, understanding, and discernment. In fact, in the absence of the practice of stillness in any realm—religious or secular—silence, wisdom, understanding, and discernment will prove largely elusive.

Need for Stillness and Silence

We were designed to desire and to need the fellowship of others, to sing, to dance, and to enjoy times of feasting. From all of these things, in appropriate times and quantity, we may be ministered to and receive something needed. Yet we are also designed to need the stillness and the silence, and from them to attain certain benefits, receive particular blessings, and be ministered to in a manner exclusively the domain of our God. For several reasons, most will recognize the reality and importance of the social and temporal facets of human design, while relatively few demonstrate any awareness of the spiritual facets that can only be engaged in stillness and silence. The problem then is that the blessings, knowledge, and understanding designed to flow into us through spiritual channels cannot be attained through any other course.

The concept is one as simple as food. The design of our bodies necessitates the ingesting of certain nutrients, vitamins, and minerals to maintain optimum health. Many foods contain an abundance of things that we need, but no single food contains all that we need. Thus we eat a variety of different foods to try to meet the multiple and sometimes varying requirements of our bodies.

The Spirit, the Soul, and the Silent Places

That which can be acquired or achieved only through stillness, as always it has been, will come only to those who master the art of stillness and wait in the practice of silence. Just as a hunter with bow ready to draw must sometimes wait, holding for long seconds, a minute, or even longer, remaining stone still and silent until that fleeting moment when a deer moves into the clear or turns his head away, only then to let fly his arrow, so, too, are the disciplines of the spirit as engaged in the silent places. Answers, understanding, and knowledge may not come quickly and often do not come when we want them. Yet so long as we hold, wait, remain still, and keep the silence, there is much that ultimately and inevitably does come.

The entirety of all that comes remains, as Theodore Roosevelt expressed, elusive of the capacity of words alone, yet the esoteric sustenance of the wild, which feeds and fortifies spirit and soul as only it can. Esoteric not because such sustenance is available only to the few but because there are relatively few who go and hold in still silence to seek it out. As in most aspects of life, so also it is with God and with the fortification of spirit and soul. What can be taken away will always correlate to the sum of that put in and given.

The vastness, the majesty, the stillness, and the calm of the silent places virtually command the processes of reflection and introspective thought. To reflect and to think introspectively are the foundational blocks of personal and spiritual growth. Apart from them, the ceiling on spiritual and true intellectual development is so low as to allow for the emergence of little genuine substance.

The unique solace of the silent places invites us to indulge in or to complete the process of mourning. Sometimes the company and support of others may be needed. At other times, it may be only the vastness, silence, beauty, stillness, and majesty of the wilderness that can minister to, and begin to heal, a spirit wounded and heartbroken.

In the Sanctuary of the Silent Places

While the believer receives ministry from all of these silent rites of the wild lands and, too, by the bold bugle of the bull elk, the plaintive cry of the fish eagle, the lone song of the wind through high mountain pines, the haunting calls of the great horned owl, or the growls and grunts of a not-so-distant lion in the night, he takes solace also in something more. Just as Job was brought to understand amid his terrible suffering, the believer is comforted in the knowledge that the same power that gave the elk his strength and voice, the lion his majesty and might, and the eagle his powerful wings and penetrating vision is the power that still holds, controls, and sustains all that is set before his eyes. Moreover, the power that closes the hands and arms holds him and his loved ones now and unto eternity.

Contemplation

The silent places beckon us toward contemplation. Of the many casualties in a modern era in which most people are absorbed—and by which they are dominated—technology, the loss of the capacity for, and even the will to pursue extensive and in-depth thought is foremost among them. The manufactured busyness, the ceaseless drone of music on headphones and in car, café, club, and home, the mindless viewing of electronic garbage and fantasy on television and computer, and the hours given to constant texting and frivolous chatter on cellular phones combine to preclude any prospect of meaningful thought. Thus we are never surprised when among youth, university students, and even some adults well into their fourth decade of life, the answers on their worldview and thoughts on significant matters commonly received are astonishing both in shallowness and brevity. They speak of little of substance because they have little substance of thought.

Many hunters, both old and young, contrary to stereotypical insinuations and depictions in media and film, can converse intelligently on virtually any subject because they have had the will, the time, and the requisite atmosphere to think about and to contemplate all things. Most hunters we know—and we are acquainted with many—converse more intelligently and carry themselves with greater class and dignity than those who mock them, protest their activities, and spew forth tirades of hate, filth, and profanity from the Internet, sympathetic media outlets, and the protests on the streets. Hunters carry themselves differently, and with a higher standard, in part because they have constantly engaged in the process of genuine thought. They have contemplated the importance of honor, decorum, dignity, truth, principles, and faith. They have contemplated resources, ecosystems, cycles of life, and human nature, and they have considered the prospect of a world in which there was no hunting, realizing the manifold and multifaceted consequences for humans, wildlife, and land that would follow. Maturity, innovation, development and progress, temporal or spiritual, cannot come abundantly, let alone in full, apart from the presence of genuine thought and a capacity for reason.

Meditation

In the sanctuary of the silent places is also to be found the supreme and untainted ground for the practices of meditation and prayer. Just as a rifle much fired or exposed to inclement weather must eventually be taken apart and cleaned and restored, so with the human spirit and mind. Mind and spirit, at times, must jettison that with which they have been burdened to be cleaned, cleared, and renewed. David wrote of such cleansing and renewal in Psalm 51:10, "Create in me a clean heart, O God, and renew a steadfast spirit in me."

The fact that meditation, for millennia, has remained such a prominent practice in so many religions and faiths would seem sufficient validation in and of itself of the dividends to be yielded. Moreover, many within the field of medical science have now allowed that the practice can contribute to the overall health of mind and body. As previously stated, we believe that humans were designed not only to benefit from being still and silent amid stillness and silence, but designed also to need the unseen and unheard fortification and communion forthcoming from the discipline of still silence. Meditations in the silent places will thus prove beneficial and rewarding for all who honor its discipline, regardless of their particular religious beliefs.

For the followers of Jesus Christ, though, the requisite fortification and the blessings attained through meditation are as profound and readily apparent as are the necessity and the mandate that we meditate. We are instructed in Joshua 1:8 to meditate upon the Scripture day and night—"so that you may be careful to do according to all that is written in it." David instructed the practice of meditation in Psalm 4:4. The writers of Psalm 119:48-78 instruct us to meditate upon the statues and precepts of the Lord. In verse 27, one perhaps overlooked by some but not likely by hunters, the writers instruct us to meditate upon the wonders of the Lord. Nowhere are the wonders of our Lord so prominent or in evidence as in the wild silent places. When we meditate upon the strength of the grizzly bear, the majesty of the bull elk, the speed of the cheetah, the leaping of the springbok, the splendor of thick-antlered Kaibab muley bucks, the regality of the kudu, the power of clashing big horn rams, the footing of the mountain goat, the grace of the giraffe, the beauty of wild mustangs in flight, the glory of the lion, the depth of the canyon, the height of a mountain, or the flow of a river, we acknowledge and reflect upon the multiplex degree to which all of these attributes are held and wielded in the mind and hands of the God who watches over, holds, and sustains us. We remember the God who, as much as He loves the magnificence of the beauty and diversity in the landscapes and creatures of His creation, loves us who are created in His image even more.

While the scriptural mandate is sufficient reason to engage in the practice of meditation, to understand the practical reasons for so doing

The Spirit, the Soul, and the Silent Places

may prove helpful. First, the God of the universe has little tolerance for petty competition—those things or behaviors that distract us from Him for significant stretches of time. Second, the nature of the world, the relentless press of the spiritual forces of evil with the fearsome power they possess—these are given the freedom of rule and utmost sway on the earth. The fallen, sinful nature borne by all of us from the blight of original sin combine with these forces to form a volatile and treacherous spiritual environment laden with uneven ground, temptations, pitfalls, snares, and volleys of enemy arrows. To pursue the path of righteousness in all things is never the easiest course. Nor is such the natural inclination of the human mind and heart.

If the ways of righteousness are not pursued deliberately with relentless perseverance, then only a matter of time remains before we fall away or abandon outright this standard. Only by keeping the statues, precepts, and wonders of our God before our eyes and in our minds can we then stand firm and prevail in righteousness in the hostile and trap-ridden environment, which exists in this world under rule of the spiritual forces of wickedness. Just as exercise and training with firearms and blade keep the body ready in case called upon to defend and as proper maintenance of weapons assures their performance, so the practice of meditation cleans, renews, and fortifies the spirit and mind so as to be prepared both for physical battle as well as the dangers and assaults surely to come in the spiritual realm.

Prayer

More often than we are instructed to meditate, we are commanded through Scripture to pray. Prayer can be a component of meditation or can be separate from it. Such is a matter of personal preference. In fact, any man who desires the blessings of God on his family and on himself is instructed in the first Psalm to meditate: "In His law he meditates day and night." But Christian meditation has little in common with yoga or other Eastern forms of meditation carried out in the lotus position and a saffron-colored robe. It is not just the contemplation of nature but rather the contemplation of the God over all nature, His Word, His plans, and His purposes. Neither is it a substitute for assembling together with God's people in church (Hebrews 10:25). But neither is corporate worship a substitute for time alone with God, and this latter is nowhere better accomplished than in the silent places.

The silent places offer a sanctuary for prayer unlike any other. They welcome specific prayers of entreaty the same as the more meditative art of contemplative prayer. For us, to venture into the silent places, in and of itself, is an act in which we feel a silent but sensory call to prayer. We find it difficult to feel the recoil of a shouldered rifle, smell the spent powder in the air, and then see the quarry fall and not breathe a prayer for the multiple gifts represented in the single, simple act. Beyond any act or purpose, though, it is simply to be in the wild majesty of the soul-soothing silence that seems to command the practice of prayer. To find a place with a pleasing view and then settle and be still usually begins a process of contemplative prayer without any previous deliberation.

Contemplative Prayer

Contemplative prayer is merely the act of thinking through—in the presence of God—the issues, problems, challenges, or questions with which you may be faced while seeking, remembering, and reflecting upon the precepts and principles of Scripture as would be applicable to each. Such prayer engaged in the silent places with introspection, open mind, and intellectual integrity often leads to realizations and understanding beyond that previously held. Because the mind and spirit are open and free from all distractions, the mind becomes more acute and efficient, moving in steady ease within the stilled body. Likewise, the Spirit of God then is active and ready to enter the door that has been opened and to move within mind and heart of the man in sacred communion. The entry and movement of the Spirit of God may bring comfort or peace. He may grant wisdom, understanding, and discernment. He may reveal answers to questions with which you have long pondered or grappled. He may bestow upon the seeker some combination of all these blessings. Such depends upon the needs of the individual in conjunction with the purposes and will of God.

Many men are uncomfortable praying aloud in a church or Bible study group around large groups of people. If you are such a man, then that is fine so long as you do not take the fact as a justification for not praying at all. You can pray alone or with trusted friends at home, in your truck, or deep within the vast reaches of the silent places. The same God who sees and hears all of His children will hear and consider a prayer lifted up from the remotest wilderness the same as one lifted from the grandest church. For some, the inclination to prayer may be more powerfully felt in the silent places, where the statutes, precepts, works, and wonders of the Lord come vividly and majestically together before mind and eyes.

Indigenous Peoples

The encounters with God and self are not the only ones to be expected if much time is spent in the silent places. When we speak of the wild, uninhabited regions, such a designation is only a partial truth. Wild, silent, and free of urban sprawl to be sure, but they are not wholly uninhabited. Indigenous tribes and peoples usually in relatively small and widely scattered populations, often live in these regions—sometimes in a way similar or the same as they have for hundreds of years or more. Another reason that the men and women who hunt extensively tend to be more widely knowledgeable and cultured than the average person who confines himself to urban and suburban centers and insulated vacation resorts is that they have encountered and interacted with many peoples and cultures upon their own ground and terms.

For us, such interaction has included Native Americans in the United States and Mexico, Masai, Samburu, Ndebele, San, Zulu, and Lunda, among many others in Africa, and Pakistani tribes in the remotest parts of that country near the Afghan border. The results in Pakistan ended in what can only be described as comedy and chaos. We laughed about it then and we still laugh today when we remember. While the deer were found, no trophies were marked except for the ear of one of the hounds running out the deer. A badly misplaced shot—intended for the deer—from the AK-47 of an overly eager but not particularly sharpshooting tribesman was the cause of the hound's wounded ear. In the melee that then ensued among the tribesmen, all armed with AK-47s and an array of blades, the deer, of course, all trotted leisurely away to the safety of cover.

The time spent interacting among diverse peoples and cultures in the silent places throughout the world becomes an education of a depth and kind unattainable in any university and unequalled by the study of books. Such represent not only the most profitable form of learning, but also the most riveting, enjoyable, and memorable kind. Further, for those so inclined, such encounters offer unique venues and opportunities in which to share the gospel of Jesus Christ—opportunities to bear testimony of the Good News of Jesus Christ to individuals not to be found in churches or church-related activities. Just as hunters enjoy the diversity of wildlife sprung forth from the creative genius of our God, so, also, can His creative genius be appreciated and enjoyed in the diversity and varied appearances and gifts of His many children.

My decision to take all my children and grandchildren to Africa has been rewarded in dozens of ways. By the time they were ten, my granddaughters could visit a zoo and name most of the animals and describe their habitats. Armour, my son, took to Africa like a Labrador retriever to a water sport. Recently in Zambia, our outfitter Pete Fisher,

The Spirit, the Soul, and the Silent Places

invited us to go with him to deliver Armour's sable to an orphanage. What a scene! One little boy of the Lunda tribe stayed to himself and quietly wept. Armour asked about the child. "Two days ago, both of his parents were killed," came the reply. I watched my boy approach the child, pick him up, hug and kiss him and set the child down in his lap. Soon he was surrounded by orphan children who just needed a hand of love. Here was my son, the outdoorsman, the hunter, loving children so far in the African bush that few white men ever see them. Frankly, we were not thinking much about the hunt right then, but it was worth every penny I spent to see that scene.

My son-in-law, Mark Howell, is one of the must unselfish hunters I have ever known. He once accompanied me to Africa and never fired a shot, pushing me and others ahead of himself, content to help and protect us. As a result, God has given him two top animals—the envy of hunters everywhere. In addition, he captured one poacher!

Intergenerational Relationships

Of all encounters that may occur within the wild, silent places of the earth, though, the one that remains the most important—after that of introspective self and the spirit of the living God—is the coming together of the knowledge and wisdom of the graying heads with the strength and passion of youth. Amid the reflection, contemplation, mourning, meditation, prayer, and cleansing and renewing of spirit and mind, all interspersed with the quest, the thrill of the chase with rifle in hand, shots fired, game taken, the rejoicing at a successful day's end, and the melancholy or frustration of game missed or never found, the encounters and meaningful interaction invariably come. Such openings need not be sought or forced. The spirit of the wild, the dynamics of the hunt, and all that is inherent to the silent places come together and work in conjunction to open the channels of communication between young and old. Innate in this communication is the frankness and honesty of it. The silent places, in a way unique and inimitable, assure the fact as only they can.

Remember that the hunt, as much as any other endeavor and far more than most, has a way of bringing forth honesty and revealing truth of character and thoughts—for better or for worse. The result of what is learned can be a positive or a negative. You may wish to hunt with a good, amiable, and thoughtful man with an irresistible sense of humor again and spend more time with him at home. On the other hand, you may not wish to see a selfish, bitter, and ill-humored man, again under any circumstances. With boys, girls, and young adults, however, the dynamics change. The truth that comes from their words and the genuine substance of their emerging and unveiling character is positive and presents a blessed opportunity, regardless of the nature of what is revealed. For the revelation of good character and inclinations puts in the hands of the older hunter a fine new blade to be sharpened, honed, and fit with a proper sheath. Conversely, the revealing of flawed character, perspectives, and wrong inclinations puts in the older hunter's hands a chunk of raw, unworked steel, which must be cut down, forged in the fire, and then formed from scratch before the sheath and any effective utilization can be considered.

Yet the older hunter must try—bringing all ingenuity of mind, strength and effort of body, the fire, the sweat, and sometimes the tears. For this is his calling and obligation as man and hunter before the Lord. While often not the case with older adults, the young are inherently more open, more impressionable, and more malleable. Upon being shown the genuine actions of love and having honor, strength, gentleness and righteousness put before them in the form of a living example and role model, they are inclined to respond and change. To impart such understanding and elicit significant change for the better, the older hunter must strive because of his calling and obligation before the Lord. He must strive with perseverance and patience because the hunt and the untamed spirit of the silent places puts him in a position of potential influence in the hearts and minds of boys and young men unparalleled by the positions of any other older men in their lives. The men who hunt with a young man share the highs and lows, the jubilance and disappointment, the hardship, the solace, the danger, the challenge, the encounter with magnificent, strange, and humorous creatures. Encounters with exotic peoples, the chase, the vastness, and the quiet are all experienced in varying degrees amid the silent places. Doors of heart and mind, for which other men—regardless of any honor of good intentions—possess neither a working key nor any mechanism by which to defeat the lock, are opened.

The suggestion is not that God does not use honorable men and women who do not hunt to influence the lives of the young for the better. Surely He can and absolutely He does. The point to be understood is that there will always be a significant percentage of boys and young men—and some young women—who will not be impressed, influenced, or reached by the common methods and offerings of the church or by society in general through soft, frivolous, often dull and politically correct offerings. Among such youth, neither pastors, youth leaders, worship leaders, teachers, coaches, counselors, motivational speakers, political leaders, celebrity athletes, nor successful business leaders will have openings to communicate and potential for positive influence comparable to that acquired by the men who ventured with them into the silent places.

If, on the other hand, boys and young men become interested in and then committed to God and the pursuit of His precepts and ways, then their commitment to and presence in the church will usually follow by way of their own convictions and volition. This approach is often more effective than one in which all aspects of church and its activities seem to be shoved down their throats. How better to interest them in

God and in the pertinence of His ways than to reveal to them the most splendid works and wonders of His hands and to share with them the unforgettable, educational, and potentially life-changing ventures into the silent places. They may then take their places in church as faithful members, leaders, and men of God.

Nevertheless, the church must do all the good, honorable, and godly things that it does. We simply add a word of caution. If churches wish to reach men and boys, they must recover ways to minister to boys and men as God made them through those masculine emphases. They need to be challenged to become godly men, protectors and providers for the weak of society.

INTERLUDE

FROM THE LAND TO THE WATERS

> When I consider Your heavens, the work of Your fingers,
> The moon and the stars, which You have ordained;
> What is man that You take thought of him,
> And the son of man that You care for him?
> Yet You have made him a little lower than God,
> And You crown him with glory and majesty!
> You make him to rule over the works of Your hands;
> You have put all things under his feet,
> All sheep and oxen,
> And also the beasts of the field,
> The birds of the heavens and the fish of the sea,
> Whatever passes through the paths of the seas.
> PSALM 8:3-8

As we transition from the land to the waters, let us again be clear that there are many activities and endeavors besides hunting or fishing that may be profitable in reaching the hearts and minds of the young, teaching them the crucial lessons of life and sustaining an influence in their lives for the better. Indeed, other activities should be engaged regardless of the amount of hunting or fishing undertaken. Further, some youth will never be enticed by hunting and fishing and will not feel the spiritual beckoning and pull of the wild and silent places. Such young people must be reached through mediums of activity, so long as they are wholesome, that most interest them.

Nevertheless, a mandate from God through the poetry of David in Psalm 8 holds some level of relevance for all men, regardless of whether or not they hunt or care to go out into the silent places. Speaking of man, David wrote, "You make him to rule over the works of Your hands; You have put all things under his feet" (v. 6). As David goes on to reveal, these things include not only the land itself but also "the beasts of the field, the birds of the heavens and the fish of the sea" (vv. 7-8).

That all of creation has been put under our feet and that we are given the charge to rule over it entails then that we are stewards of the land, the waters, and of all creatures therein. That we are all, in fact, stewards cannot be in question. The only question is whether we are good stewards or negligent ones; active stewards or apathetic ones; responsibly studied and informed stewards or willfully ignorant ones. Hunters who have been properly taught and trained carry an understanding of the concepts and requirements of responsible stewardship as well as the realization of the requisite, simultaneous roles of man as hunter, fisher, preserver, and protector in the overall process. In a democratic society, however, all people, regardless of levels of experience in, or knowledge of, wildlife and ecosystems, have a vote, and thus a say, regarding the methods of stewardship to be employed. All, then, and all believers most surely, need to possess some level of sound understanding about wild country, the seas, and the creatures therein.

As for fishing, many of the blessings and rewards to be gained thereby are the same as those taken from the hunt. Nevertheless, there are differences in the nature and execution of the two endeavors as well as some variation in what is taken from them. As will be seen, fishing, even more than hunting, is stately, purposefully, and unalterably linked to the decision and mandated path of following Jesus Christ. Fishing, too, in certain respects holds more in common with the Christian path of life than does hunting. Thus an argument could be made that all who choose to follow Jesus Christ, regardless of interest, gender, or age, should be taught or otherwise attain an understanding of the basic concepts and rudiments of fishing.

Fishing can be on the surface or under the surface. Recently in Hawaii, all my family was enjoying a few days of respite. "Let's go fishing," they demanded. A boat was engaged, and out we went. I have never been seasick or airsick throughout my traveling all over the world to more than 125 countries. So, naturally, I was game. I also held over Armour's head that he had "fed the fish" on our first outing into the Pacific in Hawaii when he was about fourteen years of age.

The fishing on this day was not bad, but the seas were about as calm as a hurricane. Since at age seventy I had never had a problem, I had taken no precaution. I can tell you that seasickness is not gradual. One second I was fine. The next, I was hung over the rail. We were about five miles out, and I spent the next three hours in that terribly uncomfortable position of literally clinging to the side of the boat. I lost everything I had eaten for the last year, or so I felt.

Amazingly, only ten feet below the surface, the waters would have been mild and the under-ocean beauty spectacular. Those who have never been down can scarcely imagine. Fields of colorful corral are accentuated by some of God's most colorful maritime creations. But even here there is adventure and danger. Lion fish, sea snakes, and even the coral itself can take a toll, including your life.

Swimming along one day in the iridescent blue waters of the Red Sea, gazing from my face mask I caught movement at about 35 feet beneath the surface. Turning, I saw the sea snake, more poisonous but less threatening than similar land specimens swimming my way.

Mysteries of the Bush

Glancing back, I discovered that he was merely the scout. Here came an army of between 50 and 100 of these creatures! How still can a man be in the water? I hardly took a weak breath and never flexed a muscle until the last snake swam past. Adventure? Dive to the depths.

Now, there is great skill in fishing. Two men go to the same place. One returns with nothing while the other totes a heavily-laden stringer. I do not deny that there is some luck as, for example, when I caught the largest silver salmon one year in Alaska. But the knowledge of fish, their habits, and habitats is a life-time learning prospect. We have the greatest admiration for gifted anglers.

CHAPTER 7

THE SANCTUARY OF THE EVERLASTING BOND

> *O Lord God of hosts, who is like You, O mighty Lord?*
> *Your faithfulness also surrounds You.*
> *You rule the swelling of the sea;*
> *When its waves rise, You still them.*
> Psalm 89:8-9

In a world increasingly dominated by crowded living, noise, technology, bustle, and busyness—both that which is real as well as that which is self-manufactured—people of all ages and both genders, more than ever before, need a place of sanctuary. Again, those denying any need of such may often be in greater need than are those admissive of the fact. Commonalities ranging from stress-induced illness and agitation to drug dependency—legal and otherwise—bills for psychiatric help, domestic disputes, road rage, spikes in juvenile violence, and a general inability of so many to cope with and resolve basic human issues. The fact that these crises have been effectively handled by most for millennia speak more poignantly to this truth than could any volume of words.

Sanctuaries for Fishing

As a young boy growing up in a heavily populated city that I hated, yearning always for the vast and open wild, silent places, the relatively nearby lakes, streams and sea were my earliest sanctuaries. They were my sanctuaries even before I was able to identify them as such and well before I could fully understand or articulate the spirit of the wild that pulled relentlessly upon my own spirit and soul. Yet on a small lake in southeast Texas and on the gulf shores with Papa Kelley; on numerous lakes, streams, and ponds with my father; far out in the Gulf of Mexico with him and my uncle David, and on church camping trips to lakes in northeast Texas with the RAs (a local church missions organization named Royal Ambassadors), I found a solace and a sustenance for spirit and soul to make more bearable the monotony, boredom, and overcrowding of urban sprawl.

On the waters there was always something to hope for and to look forward to. The noise, traffic, and dull predictability of metropolitan life could be tolerated and pushed through for the sake of the good times promised to come at lake, sea, or stream. If I waited and properly carried out my responsibilities with a good attitude, then there would be an opportunity to feel the thrilling strike of a bass, catfish, trout, crappie, or sheepshead on the end of my line. While the strike, the fight, and the number of fish I might be able to put on my stringer to bring home for the freezer—and, of course, always the dream of the ten-plus pound black bass—were all that filled my mind at the time and although it was indisputably fortifying and profitable for a young boy to experience the challenge and solace of the waters, there was something far more important unfolding.

Just as was to happen later in life through the hunt, eternal and unbreakable bonds were being forged with the men in my life, and the foundations for the imparting and receiving of knowledge, wisdom,

The Sanctuary of the Everlasting Bond

and counsel were being laid. The men who took me to my sanctuary and taught me how to catch, clean, and cook fish, and who spent—and, in some cases, "endured" might be a better choice of word—long hours with me on the water trying to find the fish and to figure out what kind of bait they were hitting, were then the men who opened the doors to my young heart and malleable mind. Again, the men exclusive to the conventional structure of city, school, and church had no key or method by which to open those doors. Learning to sing, give testimonies, exploit the mall, enjoy picnics at the park, play games, and be an exemplary student carried no weight with me, and there always will be many boys and young men for whom the same is true.

Although the dynamics of the opening of the hearts and minds of the young are essentially the same in fishing as in hunting, one important distinction should be noted. While access to the best of hunting can be dependent upon either personal associations or levels of financial expenditure not viable for some, good fishing—and especially that at a level certain to entice and thrill the young—is accessible to virtually all without any need of exotic locales or exorbitant expenditure. To share the experience and sanctuary of fishing with the young—thus opening the doors to their hearts and minds while also granting them sanctuary from the relentless press of urban sprawl and technology—fathers, grandfathers, uncles, and mentors need only to have the patience and the will to take the time.

For this reason, fishing became both my sanctuary and the catalyst for the opening of heart and mind to counsel and to the learning of the vital lessons of life long before I ever carried a rifle into the field after deer for the first time. My earliest memory is of pulling a trout out of a stream in the Ozarks when I was around three years old as my father, with one hand on the rod and one on me, assisted. The trout could not have weighed much more than a pound, yet for all of my struggle and unbridled excitement, I might as well have been a man battling a 400-pound marlin on the high seas.

From that time on, my father was always faithful in taking me out to lakes, ponds, streams, and sea to spend hours and often entire days in pursuit of fish. To my mind, there was no better or more rewarding way to spend the day. Even if we returned with only one catfish or a few small bream, I had no doubt but that the time spent and effort expended had been well worthwhile. On the few days that we came home after dark empty-handed, it never once dawned on me that our time could have been better spent in any other endeavor. Any prospect that my father was not every bit as enthralled as was I and was not having just as much fun as I was never entered my mind.

Bonding among a Grandfather, Father, and Son

Not long after the catching of the first trout, Papa Kelley, my beloved grandfather, realized my passion for fishing. There is no way that I could calculate or even guess the number of hours he spent alone with me fishing on his dock and in his boat at the little lake in southeast Texas. On a few occasions he took me out on the piers or shores in Galveston to fish for a bigger and more varied catch. Again, it surely never occurred to me that he was not just as thrilled as was I to have a line in the water or that he could have any need or desire to be doing anything else.

With the passing of years, of course, I came to realize that there were many days when both Dad and Papa would have much preferred to have been doing something else—perhaps anything else—besides sitting out on a lake for long, hot hours or entire days with a young hard-headed boy for the sake of a few small fish. I also came to understand that all of the time and effort spent to help me catch fish actually had very little to do with fishing. True, they wanted to teach me to make my way in the outdoors and to take and utilize the harvest of the waters. Important though such learning is for boys, however, it pales against the significance of the greater lessons that they intended to, and did, teach.

Dad and Papa understood that being alone with me for extended periods far away from the distractions of the city and engaging with me in an activity that I loved eventually would open my ears, heart and mind to their words in a way and to a degree that no other activity or program could duplicate. They knew that, with the bonds of time and shared experience on the quiet waters and around platters of fresh fried fish at the dinner table, I would ultimately and voluntarily speak of things that I would reveal to no others. I would bare the deepest inclinations, fears, and desires of my heart. I would ask questions that I was unwilling to ask anyone else and then would truly listen to their answers. The simple act of getting away from the confines of the city and putting lines in the water, in essence, put all matters on the table for open and honest discussion. Amid the talk, the discussions, and the arguments, in the long interludes of silence on the water, at the campfire, or in the cabin, there was then the time and the requisite atmosphere for thought, consideration, and reflection.

In remembering and reflecting upon the many days spent upon lake, pond, stream, and sea with Dad and Papa so many years ago, the formative nature and cumulative, life-changing effect of that time and shared experience becomes more vivid and revealing with each year that passes. Papa was a man very different than me in many ways, and yet his influence upon me was probably greater and more profound than that of any man in my life other than my father. He did many things to endear himself to me and continued to teach me valuable lessons throughout his life, and we never even got around to fishing together as fellow adults. Nevertheless, the bond that we held and that we carry through eternity, though fortified later by other components, was first forged on the water over submerged lines.

Likewise, between my father and me the links in the unbreakable chain an eternal bond were formed and fortified through numerous shared experiences in many places. At the age of three, with his help, I pulled the first trout out of the water. Since that time we have spent countless hours on the water from Texas up to Alaska, the Pacific Islands to the Mediterranean, and Lake Victoria to the Sea of Galilee. Thus we must conclude that our bond, too, was initially forged on the water.

From the perspective of a father, watching my son land that little trout, seeing his joy and triumph, and watching my 3-year-old begin his trek to manhood—that day was more liberating and fulfilling than had I caught a 400-pound marlin. Watching my 12-year-old son bag his first 10-point buck was more invigorating than a cold drink of water in the desert. By his side through every stage of development, I was able to see my son become a real man of God.

Royal Ambassadors

To the end of giving credit where credit is due as well as that of the hope of prompting consideration among current pastors and church leaders, I would be remiss not to note a specific contribution by the First Baptist Church of Dallas in the early years of my own life. At a time when the Southern Baptist Royal Ambassador program had begun to fade away from most churches and had long been ended in many, First Baptist Dallas was still making an effort to keep the program alive. Although the program seems to be virtually extinct in most churches, we could hope for its return in some form or another.

The chief purpose of the RA program was to teach boys and young men about the process and importance of world missions. However, another of the program's objectives, and one used as a medium whereby to teach, was to get boys and young men into the outdoors. In so doing, the program functioned as sort of a spiritually-centered version of the

The Sanctuary of the Everlasting Bond

Boy Scouts. Diverse outdoor activities were offered, such as hiking, rappelling, and camping in various locales. Participation in mission work at home or abroad and road trips to college football games were also undertaken. For me and for many of the boys, however, the camping trips to local lakes were most favored among the activities offered.

Those who had seldom been beyond the urban landscapes of their homes and city were taught the basics of making camp and outdoor survival. All were given the opportunity to fish to their hearts' content. In the evenings, all then gathered around the campfire to cook their fresh catch in the manner of their choosing. At some point each evening, there would be a brief lesson or study from Scripture and a time of prayer. To note what should be obvious, there were many boys and young men, me included, who were far more inclined to listen to and to engage the precepts and principles of Scripture within the setting of a fishing camp than there ever were in the confines of church services and Sunday School. The fishing trips and other outdoor excursions thus not only provided a sanctuary and bonding opportunity for urban-bound boys but also allowed for unique and innovative teaching opportunities—an opening for the wisdom and knowledge of the gray heads to be passed down to, and considered by, the seeking minds and hearts of the growing strength and passion of youth. So long as the modern church is going to be involved in extracurricular activities and programs, something along the lines of the old RA program would be worthy of consideration.

In fact, here is a challenge. Churches can no longer support the compromised Boy Scouts. RAs has been turned over to the good intentions of the Woman's Missionary Union. But think about that for a moment and the impossibility of the effort becomes immediately obvious. Awana is a fine program but may not have the missionary content that has characterized Southern Baptists, nor does it have the extent of wilderness training of the old scouting programs. One of the greatest needs in the church today is for some younger men to devise and produce an imaginative program that introduces boys 9 to 18 to Christian manhood. Had we another life, we would devote it to that effort. A program that teaches interested boys to hunt, fish, and make camp; to shoot rifles, pistols, and bows; to pray, learn Scripture, witness, love, be advocates of justice, and someday become loving husbands and faithful fathers would be unique in all the earth. Is someone out there willing to pursue this challenge?

Time for Conversation

In addition to being easily accessible to virtually all people, fishing has the advantage of being conducive to conversation. Many facets of hunting demand silence or the kind of movement and exertion prohibitive of many words. While fishing can just as easily provide the kind of serene sanctuary fit for reflection, prayer, and meditation, it also affords the setting for prolonged, substantive conversation between father and son, among brothers, or between friends. Such interaction between old and young can be a source of spiritual growth and learning. Between brothers or friends it can serve to encourage, inspire, work through ideas and questions, or to maintain integrity and accountability in a secure and isolated setting that inherently lends itself to introspection and honesty.

Proverbs 27:17 tells us, "Iron sharpens iron, so one man sharpens another." Thus the maintaining of a "sharpened blade" should always be a component of fishing among men regardless of the ages of those involved. On reflection, one of the regrets I carry for having lived so far from most of the cherished men in my life is the lack of opportunities to fish with them. The regret, though, really has nothing to do with the fishing, as a quick four-hour drive puts me at the shore of the Gulf of Mexico. The regret, rather, is for the loss of time together to talk through questions and problems, to reminisce, to encourage, and to hold accountable in some isolated spot on lake or river.

The Sanctuary of the Everlasting Bond

Our conversations on the water through the years have covered all aforementioned categories, and virtually every subject under the sun, in accordance with the stages of life and the specifics of character and need of those present on a given trip. In addition to the use of the water for solitude and the fortifying of spirit and soul in the still silence of sanctuary, utilize it also for the sharpening of the "iron." The fact that much of Jesus' most important interaction with His disciples occurred on the water or on the shores is not coincidence. His most famous sermon was preached in the hills just above the shores with the lake filling the background. At the center of it all were the fish (loaves and fish, for example), for the fish were ultimately the reason why most involved were present at that time and place. Yet the core of what transpired there really had nothing to do with fish. Sound familiar? More on that will be forthcoming.

Although not what you are likely to hear in Sunday School or from the pulpit of a church, the fact is that the more you fish—presuming that you do so with a reasonably active and sober mind—the more certain precepts and principles of Scripture will become clear to you. The greater the variety and locales of your fishing, still greater will be the understanding and knowledge that will come. You begin to understand more about yourself, about others, and to gain discernment with regard to the stages, rhythms, and nature of life. Then in encountering the beauty, majesty, variety, complexity, power, and awe of nature, you meet on the terms of Him whose faithfulness surrounds all, who rules the swelling of the sea, and who makes its waves rise and then stills them.

CHAPTER 8

PERSPECTIVE AND MYSTERY

*"But now ask the beasts, and let them teach you;
And the birds of the heavens, and let them tell you.
"Or speak to the earth, and let it teach you;
And let the fish of the sea declare to you.
"Who among all these does not know
That the hand of the LORD HAS DONE THIS,
In whose hand is the life of every living thing,
And the breath of all mankind?"*
JOB 12:7-10

The righteous Arab sheikh said it well again: "Let the fish of the sea declare to you," he told his friends upon their futile attempts to explain his afflictions. All who go to the sea with reasonably open, active, and sober minds indeed will see and hear both fish and mammal declare to them the power, majesty, and genius of our Lord.

THE LURES OF FISHING

Sights and Sounds

When you see a school of dolphinfish (mahi-mahi) racing at 50 mph just below the surface of the clear water on a sunny day, their iridescent gold, bright blue and green forming blurred, ever-shifting streaks glowing brilliantly within the sea, they seem as to be carrying batteries or as if plugged into some unseen source of power. In their truly splendid and electric appearance, they do, in fact, declare a power source unlike and unmatched by any other. They declare the wonder, genius, and power of the unseen hand and unfathomable mind of the living God.

When you feel the power of a marlin, sailfish, bigeye, yellowfin or bluefin tuna strike and take out the line—a force unstoppable for some time—he declares to you the power of his maker. As he breaks the surface and dances o'er the rolling, deep blue swells, his massive body glistening silver tinged with yellow or blue, he speaks of the glory and majesty of the one whose hand gave him form and life. The fact that if you make one mistake at the wrong time, he can drag you down to the cold, darkened depths of the sea that is his home—never to be seen again by any upon the earth—declares before all the temporal insignificance and frailty of men in relation to the barely middling creatures on creation's scale. This happened recently to an experienced fisherman off the Carolina coast when he got the line wrapped around his wrist with a blue marlin at the end of it.

Along these lines, the incredible force of a shark strike can be as chilling as it is thrilling, especially for those who understand, and let alone have seen, the ease with which a shark can shred the flesh of fish or man. He declares, in his own unique way, the fearsome power of his maker, reminding all that even the strongest and most brilliant of men are reduced to merely protein upon entering the water. Those who submerge as hunters inherently become potential prey.

Note our reference to "water" and not to the sea. Bull sharks have attacked, killed, and eaten people in rivers and lakes in Iran, southern Africa, and Nicaragua, among other places, at least as far as 150 miles from the nearest saltwater. Further, they have been spotted in

Perspective and Mystery

brackish and fresh water in Louisiana and well up into New York's Hudson River.

The prophet Jonah was the recipient of a lesson in both mystery and perspective, and the lesson likely came in the mouth and gut of a massive shark. Recall that the prophet's own account specifies that "the Lord appointed a great fish," not a mammal such as the commonly presumed whale. The ancient *Carcharodon*, said by experts to have been extinct now for millions of years, would seem a potential candidate. The size of the massive fossilized teeth that have been found would indicate a shark of possibly 100 feet in length. Of greater interest and quite revealing is the fact that more of these enormous teeth—much larger than those of the biggest known sharks—have continued to turn up in the fresh sediment of the sea, and they are not fossilized! Aside from the obvious implications to Jonah's experience, the fact serves as a reminder that the "experts" really have no idea what may lurk even today in the cold, darkened depths of the sea. Perhaps they, as Jonah, could take a lesson in humility, mystery, and perspective.

In a way not so menacing, the great mammals of the sea declare the glory of our Lord. In the playful schools of dolphins and porpoises jumping and racing along the bows of boats and riding the waves with surfers is declared our Lord's love of the beauties of form, grace, and symmetry. In the voice of their communications and songs is declared His brilliance and provision. From diverse cultures, from the Red Sea to the Atlantic and Pacific and beyond, in the many stories of dolphins having saved the lives of people either from drowning or from sharks—far too many and too pervasive to be disregarded—is declared the affection and love of our Lord for both His creatures and the men made in His image.

To see the bulk of a fifty-foot humpback whale cruise beneath your boat, rolling slightly to glance curiously upward is to witness the declaration of but a fraction of the magnitude of the capacities of the

Creator. Then to see him propel the whole of his 78,000 pounds out of the water as he breaches and crashes back into the blue sea declares just a hint of His power. The songs of the whales below the ocean's surface leave a haunting declaration of but one form of the vast array of music beloved of our Lord.

Then we consider the truly amazing, almost surreal, varieties of color and form amid the diverse fish inhabiting the sea's reefs. Too many to recount and too splendid, and even too bizarre, to be done justice by any attempt at words—yet they declare the Lord's love of variety, diversity, and uniqueness. They speak of a mind and genius of inscrutable knowledge and depth. Yet of all the splendor and mystery that fills the seas, we merely scratch the surface. When we go to the rivers and lakes, the endeavor is usually more for the purposes of companionship, fellowship, or mentoring and teaching, though the fish are a desired reward as we never like to come home empty-handed. When we go to the sea, however, the dynamics change a bit. Fellowship is desired and always is rewarding, and any opportunity to teach or provide counsel to the young is never neglected. The primary objective, though, is generally twofold. First, there is the yearning to see, hear, feel, and then reflect upon the declarations of the power and majesty of our God. Second—and perhaps sometimes challenging for first in priority—is the desire to catch fish, and the more and the bigger, the better.

The Mystery

We love the mystery, never knowing for certain what is going to hit the end of the line. We eagerly anticipate the fight, as there are fish of varying sizes, all of which can challenge and drain the strength of even the fittest men. One leviathan alone—a large marlin or bluefin, often drains the strength of multiple strong men by the time he is landed. We look forward to the blessing of the food, as the seas provide the largest variety of fish and, to our palates, the tastiest of the bounty to

Perspective and Mystery

be taken from the waters. Finally, we are educated and blessed by the renewal of perspective that comes in a small boat on the high swells of a powerfully rolling sea when tangling with or observing creatures more powerful than are we. The perspective is one that reminds us how small and weak we are amid and against merely the forces and creatures created and controlled by our God, let alone directly before Him. Thereby we are then reminded both of our utter dependence on Him as well as the power with which He holds and protects us in His hand. We are reminded not only of our physical limitations, but also of the marked limitations of our knowledge and understanding.

We know more about the surface of the moon, and even about that of distant Mars, than we know about what lies and moves in the deepest, darkened realms of the sea. Our men have walked upon the surface of the moon and taken photographs there. The views were clear and quite spectacular. Our vehicles and cameras are presently rolling around on the vast desert surface of Mars, giving us clear pictures of what is and is not there.

Conversely, our men cannot walk the ground at the deepest depths of the sea. If they could traverse there, they still would see or learn very little in the pitch blackness. They would see only what was close around them, for such would be all that was allowed even with the aid of the most potent lighting.

The latest attempts to explore the greatest depths of the sea, though admirable, have yielded little knowledge or understanding save for a firm reminder of our limitations. With the protection and vision of the most advanced and secure deepwater submarine produced by enormous expenditure and the highest technology, the last foray into one of the ocean's deepest realms proved to be short-lived due to the dangers of the extreme pressure brought to bear upon any machine attempting to challenge such depths. Not surprisingly, the minimal images captured left us with still not much more than our imaginations to conjure up all that might be there.

Myriad Mysteries

The mysteries of life and of the universe are myriad. There are mysteries of land and sea, of stars, planets, and distant galaxies, of iniquity, the spiritual forces of evil, and of God. Always the mysteries have been; and though our learning and knowledge will grow, the mysteries will remain. Reason and logic of the sound, open mind alone should be sufficient to confirm the fact. Moreover, it is a fact confirmed quite clearly in Scripture.

Of the living God, Isaiah 45:15 states, "Truly, You are a God who hides Himself, O God of Israel, Savior!" Of man's efforts to discover the knowledge of the mysteries of land, sea, and firmament, Solomon wrote in Ecclesiastes 8:16-17: "When . . . I saw every work of God, *I concluded* that man cannot discover the work which has been done under the sun. Even though man should seek laboriously, he will not discover; and though the wise man should say, 'I know,' he cannot discover." Of wisdom and understanding, the righteous Arab sheikh observed in Job 28:20-21:

> "Where then does wisdom come from?
> And where is the place of understanding?
> "Thus it is hidden from the eyes of all living
> And concealed from the birds of the sky.

The mysteries will then remain, for this is the will of the omniscient and omnipotent God. He is a God who has hidden Himself as well as the ways and methods by which He created and controls all things. Yet His salvation, peace, comfort, and direction He will freely give to all who are open and willing to receive them. Likewise, the wisdom, discernment, understanding and knowledge

Perspective and Mystery

that can come only from Him, He will give to all in accordance with their capacities and the necessities of the path and challenges before them, though with all given being commensurate to the individual's degree of openness and effort.

To go out upon or into the sea is to be reminded of the perpetual mystery. The sea itself and the fish and mammals therein will declare to you the mystery. Yet they also will declare the majesty, power, love, and provision of Him who is "with you and will keep you wherever you go," and who "will neither slumber nor sleep" (Genesis 28:15; Psalm 121:4). The sea and its creatures declare to us that while we can never know all things, we can know that there is no greater power than that of Him who holds us in His hand and watches over us. They declare to us His sense of humor and His love of all that is beautiful. In glory and life-sustaining provision, they declare to all His actions of love toward us. Finally, they announce to all that He who is manifested in such majesty and glory in a world under the curse of sin, marred by the neglect, blight, and destructive courses of man, can, in our eternal home free us from the surrounding ravages of sin and envelop us in beauty, glory, and majesty unimaginable until we cross over and set our eyes thereon for the first time.

Whether reflecting and contemplating on flat seas, being jarred to realizations and thoughts while you struggle just to keep your feet as the boat rises, rolls, and drops on high swells, or matching muscle against muscle as you struggle against both the power of the sea and that of a great fish therein, you encounter the mystery as it is declared to you in manifold ways. The realization of the mystery, however, begets perspective. Of all that has been lost by so many in the modern technology-driven and entertainment-obsessed culture so nauseatingly bent on self-gratification, the loss of or failure ever to attain perspective may be the most profound and telling casualty. When perspective is lost, virtually all else is lost with it. If perspective is never attained, then it becomes unlikely that much else of substantial and lasting value will be gained.

Many in our great nation seem to think that their lives are terribly difficult, lacking, and oppressed. They do not have all that they think they should have. They have not been given all that they believe they are entitled to receive. Many believe that they suffer under hardship and stress.

Need for Perspective

Among the many things so obviously lacking is an understanding of how the majority of people ever to pass through this world over millennia have lived—of how little they had in terms of material things, freedom, amenities, medical care, transport, justice, or opportunity in comparison with that available to a majority of Americans today. Furthermore, most in the angry and dissatisfied crowd appear to hold neither the knowledge nor understanding of the truly difficult and, in some cases, dire conditions under which so many live in other parts of the world even today. What is lacking, in a word, is perspective.

In the absence of perspective, you cannot see what you have that is good and blessed. Without perspective, likewise, you cannot discern what is bad, what is harmful, what is unnecessary, or the lack of what is truly needed. The more that people confine themselves to the familiarity, comforts, distractions, and ease of their cities, and to the fantasy worlds of electronics, Internet, and entertainment, the more elusive perspective will become. Likewise, the less they challenge themselves physically, mentally, and spiritually, the less likely it then becomes that they will attain anything approaching a sound and well-rounded perspective. For perspective is not only requisite to the attainment of earthly understanding and knowledge. To find God and

Perspective and Mystery

to understand your place in the world before Him and among men, perspective is essential.

More than a few times men have said that they have everything that they need and want and thus have no need for God. Everyone is free to make his own choice, as our God would have it no other way. Nevertheless, what is plainly absent is a genuine understanding of the frailty and innately terminal condition of the human body, the limitations and vulnerability of all human systems, economies, and endeavors, and the utter dependence of the human soul. What is lacked then ultimately, again in a word, is perspective. With the presumed security of wealth, the abundance of ease, the amenities and pleasures of constant luxury, and the presumption of absolute safety amid seemingly secure dwellings, work places, and routes of travel, it becomes easy for some to feel invulnerable. Yet life for all people, regardless of condition, wealth, or status, is inherently vulnerable. Earthly life, by definition, is terminal. The question is not that of *if* you will breathe your last but rather that of *when* you breathe your last. The only certainty is that the time of an earthly sojourn is short and fleeting. Although not necessarily essential to the gaining of perspective, nonetheless, those who endure greater hardship expose themselves to the most powerful forces of nature, take more risks, and are more frequently exposed to danger are more likely to be intimately acquainted with the innate fragility of man, his systems, and his endeavors. Thus they are more likely to attain at least some level of perspective.

View from a Boat

The point to be taken is not that you must go out to sea or engage the struggle with a great fish in order to find salvation or truth. Nevertheless, all who are able should go out to sea and be tossed about on the mighty swells in a small boat. All who can should put a line in the water, await the strike, and then contest the strength of a great fish.

Why? Because if you go with mind and heart open, the sea will speak to you of its untold mystery. It will make known and unveil its incomprehensible power. In so doing, it will tell you of Him who rules the swelling of the sea, who makes its waves rise and then stills them. It will reveal to you, without words and as only the sea can, Him "who enclosed the sea with doors when, bursting forth, it went out from the womb" (Job 38:8).

Then the fish of the sea, in their variety, color, splendor, and speed will declare to you the omniscient genius of their Maker. The breaching whale will declare His magnitude. The great fish that takes your line and runs, unstoppable for a time, then to fight to the end until your own strength is sapped, will declare to you a power far greater than his or yours—a power immeasurable, inimitable, and insurmountable.

The sea and all creatures therein declare to you mysteries that you cannot know and were not meant to know. They declare to you a mind and power that you cannot comprehend. Yet they declare also the God "who blesses you with blessings of heaven above" and "blessings of the deep that lies beneath" (Genesis 49:25). They declare a God who, knowing all things, knows you. They declare a God who, seeing all things even unto the blackened depths of the sea invisible to us, sees you at all times. They declare a God who, by testimony of the power made manifest in them, surely holds the power to keep you, protect you, and carry you to your eternal home in His glory. At last, they declare to you a God who, having set around you beauty and majesty and provided you with abundant sustenance from sea and land, desires a relationship with you. They reveal the living and active God with whom you may enter into covenant, commune, walk day by day, and then dwell for eternity in a land and home of peace, beauty, and majesty surpassing all that has been seen or imagined. In declaring to you the mysteries of the depths, the splendor at the surface, and the power that made and holds it all, they grant to the open heart and mind the perspective of the everlasting—of Him whose "goings forth are from long ago, From the days of eternity" (Micah 5:2).

CHAPTER 9

THE BOUNTY

So when they got out on the land, they saw a charcoal fire already laid and fish placed on it, and bread. Jesus said to them, "Bring some of the fish which you have now caught."
John 21:9-10

In a fallen world where man must compete with the elements and natural obstacles of nature to attain the protein and nutrients necessary to survive, the bounty of the waters remains— as from the beginning— one of the most profluent, far-reaching, and vital blessings of our Lord upon His wayward children. Most, when imbibing of some delicacy or staple of the world's waters, will not see themselves as having challenged the elements and barriers of nature in order to obtain it—and for good reason. Most have not gone to any effort to secure such protein. Yet for every can of tuna popped open; each filet of smoked, wild-caught salmon savored; every succulent crab leg bitten into; and every wild-caught creature of river, lake, and sea plated in restaurants, someone has in fact challenged the elements and overcome nature's often formidable barriers in order to secure the vital protein for sale and consumption.

Wild-Caught Bounty

The Professionals

Apart from the blessing of provision from our Lord and the will and skills of fishermen who constantly go to sea for extended periods of time, the food supply of the world would be quite different both in variety and in the lesser quantity of wholesome protein to be had. Professional fishing can range from being monotonous, physically and mentally challenging, and exciting, to being extremely dangerous. In some of its forms, commercial fishing is continually rated as one of the world's most dangerous professions—one in which the risk of severe injury or death remains imminent. This danger is due chiefly to the harsh elements and conditions of the sea where certain creatures of the deep must be sought, as well as to the methods that have to be employed to take them. When you pay a high price for crab legs, as well as some other types of seafood, you can be certain that whoever procured your dinner surely earned his keep.

Precious Food Supply

Amid advances of modernity and due to the actions of men, both deliberate and consequential, the blessing of the bounty of the waters has become ever more precious. With the aforementioned pollution of the food chain—all that is being put into domestic stock directly as well as through the chemical poison being ingested through their food supply—the wild-caught protein from the waters has become all the more desired and valuable. And whenever possible, whether from the market or taken by your own hand, one does well to procure only wild-caught seafood or freshwater fish. The excessive pollution of the food supply for creatures raised for human consumption is not exclusive to the land. Especially in China and in parts of Southeast Asia, farm-raised fish (frequently found in American markets and restaurants) are fed variations of toxic slop, which the wise will want to avoid. The wide availability of wild-caught seafood ensures that most people, even if they do not hunt or fish themselves, can keep a staple of lean, organic protein in their diets.

To be sure, oceans, lakes, and rivers can be, and have been, polluted just as has much of the land. To do all within their power to prevent such abuse of our precious waters worldwide should be an objective of all responsible people as stewards of the sustaining lands and waters entrusted to us by our God. Avid fishermen are more conscious of the obligation and necessity than are most. Desiring that there always be plenty of fish to catch and that the purity of their food source not be compromised, they have a vested interest in conserving fish and in keeping the water clean. All who enjoy dining upon the bounty of the waters should share the same commitments toward preserving and protecting. In an urbanized and disconnected western world increasingly hostile to hunting and fishing, just as hunters put in the highest individual monetary sums contributing to the funds by which wild lands and wildlife are protected and maintained, so do sport fishermen pay the highest individual prices for the protection of the waters and its creatures. They pay all of the fees requisite for any who take a boat onto the water, but they also must pay for fishing licenses and all other associated taxes and fees. Again, hunting and fishing go hand in hand with, and are inherently inseparable from, conservation.

Seafood Markets

When in the islands or Keys, on the gulf coast, or when we descend from the high desert down to the Pacific coast, my wife Rachel and I frequently go to our favorite seafood markets and purchase quantities of the freshest local catch. Nevertheless, we never let pass any opportunity to go onto lake or river or to go out to sea to take our own fresh catch. Among the wonderful aspects of fishing are many varied and diverse opportunities to do so worldwide. The streams, rivers, lakes, and shorelines of North America, many engulfed by silence and great beauty, abound with a tremendous variety and quantity that may be harvested. Our blessed bounty from both the freshwater and saltwater of the south and southwest, Mexico, Canada, and Alaska has been diverse and tasty. From the waters of Africa, Asia, the Mediterranean, and the Aegean, we have taken a varied harvest on trips that were not even fishing trips. The fact that we always carried a rod, extra line, and hooks was sufficient to allow for such unplanned excursions.

While purchasing fresh seafood in markets is a viable option in many places, no method of procurement is so desirable and satisfying as to take the bounty of the waters with your own hands. First of all, doing so is more fun than a trip to the market, allowing for the challenge, the thrill and exertion of the fight, the fortifying companionship of family or friends, the solace of the silence or that of the loud, rolling, and crashing sea—the only sound so loud that it drowns out all other sounds and yet is soothing to spirit and mind. Second, to go upon the waters, should you so choose, offers the opportunity to encounter and fellowship with God through the experiencing of the power, beauty, and majesty that will be manifested all around you. Third, when fish are taken by your own hands, you can know with certainty the purity of the source of the catch—that your vital protein, indeed, is organic and not the product of some murky soy-laden and toxin-infested farm. When you then prepare the catch for the table, you can know that none of the processed soy, hydrogenated oils, multiple forms of MSG, or artificial sugars that fill the kitchens and desecrate the food in the bulk of American restaurants will adulterate the gifts of protein of which you and your family will partake.

Fellowship of the Day's Catch

Furthermore, no experiences have been more satisfying, and no memories remain sweeter, than the times spent with my fathers, brothers, friends, and with my wife Rachel around a fire, in a rustic kitchen, in beach bungalows, or even on the hotel room balconies of seaside resorts eating our fresh catch as we relived the day's events and conversed about all things under the sun. The main course has been black bass, crappie, bream, catfish, and trout, among others, while encamped on shores of lake or stream. Tilapia from Lake Victoria and the Sea of Galilee has gone into the skillet. In an open air bungalow on the blue and jade-colored waters of the gulf, Rachel and I have savored grilled and fried dolphinfish (mahi-mahi), various snappers, and Almaco jack taken together in the Atlantic off the Florida Keys. In both seaside cottage and resort, we have dined for days upon sashimi and poké of freshly-caught yellowfin, bigeye, and skipjack tuna taken together off the coast of Hawaii. All that is needed for these simplest yet most delicious of delicacies is a knife, small cutting board, soy sauce, wasabi for the sashimi, or a few onions, some dried seaweed, sesame oil, Sriracha sauce, and sea salt for the poké. These are but some of the water's bounty with which we have been blessed.

Those living on or near the extensive American coasts are blessed with an ever-present opportunity to take the wild-caught bounty of the sea with their own hands. Those living inland are blessed with the manifold bounty of lake, river, and stream. For the purposes of obtaining organic, unadulterated protein, sharing meaningful time with loved ones, and encountering the living God in the glory and peace of His sanctuary, opportunities to take and to share the harvest of the waters should not be neglected.

Spiritual Bounty

As substantial as are the temporal blessings to be had in fishing and as profound as are the spiritual blessings attainable both for the individual and between friends and families young and old, the extent of the spiritual side of fishing goes well beyond the bonds and realms of brothers, friends, and families as will begin to become evident. For from the spiritual sides of fishing there extend dimensions unique and beyond even the spiritual implications and blessings attainable through hunting. For all who would profess to follow Jesus Christ, striving to live by His ways to fulfill His commands, the lessons to be learned in, and the spiritual implications of, fishing must be an integral component of the understanding and practice of faith.

At Jesus' Command

After Jesus had been crucified, had risen from the grave, and then manifested Himself to His disciples on two occasions, Peter went back to his home ground on the shores of the Sea of Galilee. He and several other disciples, at least some of whom were fellow fishermen, did something wholly understandable to all who know the solace of the waters. They went out into their sanctuary.

Having endured the most traumatic period of their lives, days ridden with fear, uncertainty, and ultimate questions, they surely needed some quiet time alone among only trusted brothers to regroup and to refortify their spirits and minds. Perhaps they also needed simply to eat or to make some money. They knew the place where all could be accomplished. Not sure as to whether Roman soldiers or the leaders of the Jews might be coming for them and unsure as to exactly what their futures might hold, they went out into their sanctuary. Peter said, "I am going fishing" (John 21:3), and the others replied that they would go with him.

Collecting their nets and getting into their boat, the disciples went out onto the lake on one of those days when the water's surface was still and inviting. They fished long and hard but caught nothing. There likely were long periods of silence as each man reflected, contemplated, searched his soul, and pondered the questions of the days to come. Surely also conversation included questions asked, opinions given, and encouragement offered. Prayer, either in silence or openly as a group,

The Bounty

must have been spontaneous as they tried to discuss how and where to proceed with the rising of the morning sun. Unbeknownst to them, they were soon to know precisely their mission and course from that time and place forward with an appointed time for everything—a time for every event under the sun. Their immediate task was to be much simpler than the answering of the many questions that had filled their minds and been set forth in their words, and the soul-cleansing comfort and fellowship they had sought upon the water was to become much sweeter.

As morning's first gray light dawned over the eastern hills after a long and fruitless night of fishing, a man called out to them from the shore. "Children, you do not have any fish, do you?" They affirmed that they had caught nothing.

"Cast the net on the right-hand side of the boat and you will find a catch," the man commanded. Upon following the instructions, the men quickly had so many fish in their net that they were unable to haul it into the boat. John then realized and informed Peter that the man on the shore was Jesus Himself.

Peter, whether for better or for worse, was never a man to engage in halfway measures. As soon as he realized that the man on the shore was his Lord Jesus, he donned his outer garment and plunged into the water to make his way ashore as quickly as possible, leaving to the rest of the men the slow, arduous task of hauling in the massive catch of fish. Once all had reached the shore, they soon realized that preaching, giving admonishment and counsel, or issuing instructions were not the foremost objectives on Jesus' mind.

At Jesus' Invitation

At the Lord's feet a charcoal fire burned with fish already laid upon it. Off to the side lay a stack of fresh bread. Jesus' only instruction was for them to bring some of the fish that they had just caught over to the fire. Every man was to have his fill—not only of fresh fish and bread to satisfy the hunger of the body but also of the companionship and fellowship to feed spirit and soul.

The actions taken here by Jesus are more significant than is commonly realized. For the act of sharing a meal together in the culture of the land and times of the Bible connoted much more than does the same act in our current culture and land. To prepare a meal for others and then invite them to partake was to extend an offering of friendship and peace among all present. To eat together, then, was to be at peace with one another and to recline in the embrace of friendship.

Some may question as to why Jesus would have any need to reassure His most loyal and trusted followers of peace and friendship between them, but the answer should be apparent. The disciples knew that Jesus was aware of the doubt and faltering faith, which, against all efforts to believe and to obey, had filled their minds and hearts. Furthermore, they remembered all too painfully that some had not stood by Him to the end, and that at least one among them had denied Him and fled away. They could not know for sure exactly where they stood before Him and what His disposition toward them was ultimately to be.

The freshly-caught fish roasting over the charcoal fire hinted of a sweet answer to their questions. The heavy catch in their net and then the command to bring more fish to the fire, gather close, and prepare to eat, answered the questions in full. Friendship and peace would still be among them. Despite all that had happened in minds and hearts and in actions and words, His love and trust toward them remained unchanged. So, too, did His plans for them. The plans would be revealed soon enough. For now, though, they would merely recline, eat, and converse. They would linger and relax with little more objective than that of relishing the taste and satisfying fill of the catch and enjoying the companionship and fellowship of brothers around the fire.

The Bounty

Jesus knew people of both genders and at every stage of life with a fullness of understanding available only to the living Creator and God. Thus He understood the deep-seated needs of men, knowing that there was not—and never would be—any substitute for the simplest, holistic pleasures of companionship and nature. He knew that, along with the study of Scripture and daily interaction with Him, nothing would keep a man sharp in spirit, mind, and body in the same way as would the continual, active presence of good men at his side. No pleasure was more begetting of peace, contentment, and the inclination toward introspective reflection than was a good fire at the water's edge or in the depths of the wild, silent places. He knew that no act among men was more subtly satisfying than to savor fish or game taken together around the circle of the fire with trusted brothers or friends and none more conducive to honest and substantive interchange. He also knew that none other could be more suited to the provision of spiritual healing or fortification when needed. None provided a better medium or expression of peace and friendship among men. Thus in providing and cooking the fish and in the invitation to recline, eat, talk, and linger around the fire, Jesus acted to reassure trust, friendship, and peace; to extend spiritual healing and fortification; and to set the stage for the introspective thought, soul searching, and interchange that would culminate in an embarkation upon the most penetrating, far-reaching, and influential mission and literary endeavors of all time.

The outset of the ministry that would change the world forever came upon the waters of the Sea of Galilee with a large catch of fish (Luke 5:1-11). The initiation of the journeys and missions that were to shake the foundations of the world in every facet, bringing to countless millions peace, life abundant, and life eternal commenced over fresh-caught, roasting fish around a small fire on the shores of the same lake. The simple pleasures would remain and be enjoyed the same. The disciples would still be fishing, with all concepts, principles, and methods therein still to be utilized. The fish to be caught and the seas upon which they were to be sought out, however, were about to change.

CHAPTER 10

FROM FISHERMEN TO FISHERS OF MEN

*"Now as Jesus was walking by the Sea of Galilee,
He saw two brothers, Simon who was called Peter, and
Andrew his brother, casting a net into the sea; for they were
fishermen. And He said to them, "Follow Me,
and I will make you fishers of men."*
MATTHEW 4:18-19

Jesus, in His three fast-moving years of ministry, did not do or say anything without reason. His actions and words were for those whom He was addressing at the time, but in His omniscience and with His ultimate plan for the world and for all people who would pass through it, those actions and words were also directed toward all who would follow in the centuries and millennia to come. Thus when Jesus called out to Peter and Andrew from the shores of the Sea of Galilee with the succinct command and explanation, "Follow me, and I will make you fishers of men," the concepts and principles of fishing at once were established as a primary component of the core of the faith, relationship, and mandate, which, from that point on, was to be carried by all men and women professing to follow Him.

Fishers of Men

What this means in the life of every believer, regardless of where you live, what you do for a living, or which church you attend, is that the whole of your mandate and obligation as a follower of Christ cannot be fully understood or carried out apart from a clear understanding of the concepts of fishing. For fishing, in many ways—and particularly in the field of reaching others with the gospel of Jesus Christ—is even more like life than is hunting. As we are aware that this is a message not likely heard by many, let us present the case clearly.

You can have absolutely no knowledge of fishing; you can never have put a line in the water in your life; and you can still come to Christ and receive His salvation. You can even lead others to faith and salvation in Him while knowing nothing of fishing. Indeed, some would argue our assertion based upon their own knowledge of, or experience with, men and women who know nothing of fishing and yet have drawn many others to the saving grace of Christ. The fact is that we know many such brothers and sisters in Christ ourselves. May God bless them for their commitment and zeal.

The objective, though, as stated and then exemplified first by Jesus Himself and then by Peter, Paul, and the devoted disciples and followers, is not merely to accomplish some, or even to accomplish much with regard to drawing men to the salvation of our Lord. The objective, rather, is to accomplish the absolute most that can be achieved in your place and time with the talents, capacities, and opportunities that God has given you. Just as the fisherman usually endeavors to catch as many fish and as big a fish as he possibly can, so the objective should be the same among committed fishers of men. Your potential as a fisher of men, and thus your catching of men, will be maximized with an understanding of the concepts of fishing.

From Fishermen to Fishers of Men

We have been associated with many, ministers and laypeople alike, who have led significant numbers of people to faith and salvation in Christ. Yet the same individuals, while in the presence of non-Christians who were willing to listen and to talk—and often were eager to do so—have failed to convince or even to move just as many or more. In fact, they have prompted many to turn decidedly away merely with their opening words and manner, well before any matters of substance could be discussed.

Such reactions on the part of unbelievers generally are not due to any lack of faith or commitment on the part of the one bearing witness for Christ. The reactions come, rather, because the one who bears witness has little or nothing working for him except for faith and commitment. He is unaware of what kind of "fish" he is trying to engage. If he knows what kind of "fish" he is pursuing, then he is unaware of where and how it swims and of what it feeds upon. He may be trying to hook a mahi-mahi or a wahoo, which feed near the water's surface and hit fast-moving baits, with a still bait for grouper 300 feet below. Sometimes the proclaimer of the gospel fails to realize even what kind of water he is in. He is hoping to hook a marlin near the surface of the open sea with a pole, bait, and method by which he has caught countless catfish in some murky lake.

To catch fish, you must first know the water that you are in or on. Then you must know the nature, patterns, and feeding habits of the fish being sought. You must know the depths, temperature, and characteristics of the water they prefer. Based upon all of this, you must know what kind of bait they are likeliest to strike. Then you must have a pole, line, and hook strong enough to hold them. Finally, you must know how to work them once hooked, so as to minimize the chances of a broken line or of the fish getting free of the hook. When bow fishing, spear-fishing, or seining, the basic principles of knowledge remain the same. So it is also in fishing for men.

The Analogy of Fishing

That Jesus used the analogy of fishing to elucidate what was to be the primary purpose and sustained course of action on the part of those who followed Him never can be relegated to circumstance or happenstance. For to become fishers of men was His instruction not only to Peter and Andrew as they cast nets from their boat but also to the millions of believers who would follow throughout the uttermost parts of the earth. The analogy of fishing was one that He specifically chose for the fulfillment of His purposes. The command to prepare to go fishing for men made clear the fact that the kingdom the Lord would establish was not to be territorial and would not be defined by political power and gain. Nor was it a kingdom to be founded by military force.

Opposition

Through the analogy of fishing, Jesus revealed that the battle to be fought—to be engaged by every true believer—was a spiritual battle for the souls of men. As part of an already long-running war, the battle would pit the satanic forces of evil—the spiritual forces of wickedness in the heavenly places—against the righteousness and power of the living God as harnessed and employed by His people. That the words of Jesus' call to Peter and Andrew, and thus to us, were so few, giving only one command ("Follow Me") and one objective (become "fishers of men"), and that He alluded to only one battle serves to signify the gravity of the stakes resting in the balance upon the spiritual battlefields. The stakes were nothing less than the immortal souls of all people. As Peter soon would learn and later would write, our Lord Jesus is one "not wishing that any should perish but for all to come to repentance" (2 Peter 3:7).

Some have argued, as others will surely continue to assert, that the concept of fishing for men, of bearing witness to the saving grace and salvation of Jesus Christ and winning souls for His kingdom—is a uniquely New Testament concept meant only for certain individuals in possession of a certain gift or set apart by a particular calling. Such an assertion, though, is biblically unsupportable and wholly errant. King Solomon wrote in Proverbs 11:30, "He who is wise wins souls." Furthermore, nowhere is bearing witness listed as an option or as some sort of spiritual gift. If the purpose and objective as stated by Jesus to Peter and Andrew in Matthew 4:19 is not clear enough, then His final command as related in Matthew 28:18-20 should settle the matter.

Once you have made the decision to follow Christ, you are then to prepare for a lifetime of fishing. The most important battles for all believers—and the only ones of eternal consequence—are those for the souls of men in the ongoing war between evil and good. Ultimately, these are the only battles that truly matter even for unbelievers, for they are the only ones with eternal ramifications.

Curriculum

A successful fisherman will have had to learn about the climate, waters, and fish that he intends to catch, as well as to be knowledgeable about the equipment and tackle necessary to get to the fish, prompt them to strike, and bring them in. Likewise, an effective fisher of men will have much to learn, and the learning will be a lifelong process without end. He must know Scripture, a constant and unending task in and of itself. Then he must understand the different kinds of people—their beliefs, characteristics, inclinations, intellects, and levels of learning and knowledge. He must know something of the cultures in which they live or from which they have come. He must understand the religious beliefs, philosophies of life, and worldviews to which they are inclined. He must know the circles in which they move, the nature of their associations, and the factors, pressures, or events most formative or influential in their lives. Only when holding such understanding can a fisher of men expect to acquire the knowledge, skills, and savvy to "fish" effectively.

Mysteries of the Bush

The reason that the aforementioned people of sound faith and commitment sometimes are ineffective in communicating the gospel to others lies chiefly in their inability to recognize or to understand fish and water. You fish with different baits and methods for different kinds of fish within the same waters. When moving from river or lake to the sea, the changes in equipment, bait, and method are yet more pronounced.

You do not catch black bass in the same way that you catch bottom-scavenging catfish. You will not hook a surface-hitting wahoo while dangling a bait near the bottom for grouper. You surely will not land a marlin with the pole, line, and bait that have brought home hundreds of freshwater crappie.

Just because God has called you to a simple faith does not mean that He wishes for you to remain of simple mind. Though some may not be gifted with the capacities for refined intellects, all, if willing, can cultivate the virtues of wisdom, discernment, and understanding. Just as some levels of intelligence and the wisdom of accumulated experience must be utilized to catch fish in the varied waters of the world, so must the same be put to effect in fishing for men in the diverse environments in which they live and from which they come.

Many faithful and committed Christians over the years, eager to share their faith and to bear witness of the saving grace of Christ to others in accordance with the Great Commission and the call to be fishers of men, have presented the gospel in ways inappropriate for the setting and have used the same words to every person whom they engage. They give little or no thought to the culture or country in which they speak, even though cultures are diverse and very different even within the borders of the United States. Aside from differing ethnicities, among those of similar heritage, the north is different from the south as well as the east is from the west. Those who think not of country or culture also fail to reckon with the varying religious backgrounds, beliefs, worldviews, levels of intellect, and degree of education among the people whom they wish to draw towards the gospel light. They have eliminated the prayer for the Holy Spirit to guide them in this life-saving work.

Just as a fisherman should not expect to land a 10-pound black bass using a method and bait suited for catfish or to hook a yellowfin tuna with a still bait hanging deep for grouper, a fisher of men should not expect a university professor or an experienced, worldy-wise businessman to respond favorably to the same language, message, or manner that he may have found to be appealing among the homeless in urban shelters or soup kitchens. A fisher of men should not expect mature adults to be impressed by or responsive to a message and style designed to appeal to youth. He should not expect a deportment, style, and message that was well received by a group of southern California surfers to be of the same effect on a devout Yemenite Muslim. If he approaches a Pittsburg steel worker who has never darkened the doors of a church with the same manner and wording that he used to draw a spiritually rebellious southern man raised in the church back to God, then the steel worker is, at the least, going to be quite confused.

Tough to Catch

Respected religious leaders of any faith are always a difficult "fish" to hook, and to go out in pursuit thereof is a "fishing" trip with a low-percentage success rate to begin with. Failure by the fisher of men to understand that religious leaders must be approached and addressed differently than laypeople will guarantee an empty-handed return. As an effective fisher of men, you must know how to show politeness, respect, and deference in accordance with a given culture and the person or people to whom you speak. You must know how to speak and to reason in conformance with their customs and levels of education and knowledge.

Even the most innocent and seemingly insignificant of errors in word can prove to be an impediment in fishing for men. In a fishing camp full of non-Christian southern men, we can come to the fire and say, "Boys, let's talk about Jesus." Yet a similar address by a missionary friend of ours in Africa landed him in trouble. Some time passed before he was able to figure out how he had so offended them and why they were upset with him. As it turned out, he had simply uttered the phrase, "Let's go, boys," on the way to a Bible study. Being men, and taking very seriously both their manhood and any verbal reference to it, they had taken offense. Fortunately, the missionary made the error first among pastors and not while sharing the gospel with unbelievers.

We know many brothers in Christ in academia—in archaeology, science, philosophy, and theology, for example—who effectively shine the light of the gospel and fish for men as few others could. This they do among men inherently difficult to reach, and among men who are inaccessible to and unreachable by most others. Other men and women do the same in the fields of medicine, business, politics, and entertainment. Such men and women are often criticized by fellow believers, most of whom fall at some point along the line. They are accused of not being sufficiently aggressive or assertive in proclaiming their faith and seeking conversions. They are criticized for their caution with, and selective use of, words. They are asked why they are not passing out tracts as they move through the halls or verbally presenting the plan of salvation at every lull in conversation.

Such accusations and assertions are as ridiculous as they are unwarranted and errant. The fact is that these men and women understand well all that is entailed in being effective fishers of men. They know the "waters" upon which they move, and they know the nature and patterns of the "fish" therein. They know that they cannot adopt the methodology and phrasing of a street preacher in downtown Houston or a missionary in the Sao Paulo ghettos and retain any chance of reaching their colleagues with the gospel message. Further, they are wiser than to attempt to measure their success or standing before the Lord by the quantity of spiritual scalps taken and festooned upon the sacred pole. Their live wells, coolers, and stringers, in fact, are never full with "fish." For the "fish" in their "waters" are among the rarest and most difficult to catch. We should note, though, that an old fisherman who landed a massive blue marlin, scoring high in the record book, once returned to the Honolulu docks with his coolers empty and no stringer to fill. Yet he had in tow a marlin bigger than his boat. So the tension is between accepting the Great Commission as a mandate for every Christian to witness, while accepting such an important assignment with a mind set on preparing spiritually and mentally to do that task in the most effective way.

Fishing or Catching?

When Jesus called Peter and Andrew from the shore, He did not say, "Follow Me, and you will become fishers of men." He said, "Follow Me, and I will make you fishers of men." Jesus used the phrase "I will make you fishers of men" because He knew that to be able to fish for men effectively, the two fishermen had much to learn. The knowledge necessary to be an effective fisher of men can be broken down into three general categories. First, the basic concepts of fishing, and all entailed therein, must be understood. These Peter and Andrew knew well already. Second, the knowledge of the Word of God—part of which was already written and part of which Jesus was still to give within their lifetimes—must be attained. Third, the knowledge of people in their diversity of character, inclination, belief, intellect, education, and culture must be acquired.

Bobby Welch may very well have been using an analogy from long ago, but I first heard it from him. He said, "Teach your people to love fishing rather than catching. If they love fishing, they will catch, but if they love only catching, they will never really love fishing." Wise words from a seasoned fisherman.

We all must bear witness, fishing for men in the realm in which God has placed us and with the abilities and capacities with which He has gifted us. In fishing for men, neither any "fish" nor any "waters" is of greater import or significance than another. The importance, honor, and value of all who fish for the souls of all kinds of men is the same. To fish from the pulpit of a grand church, from the halls of highest academia, or from the inner city streets all are noble endeavors in accordance with the call of our Lord Jesus, and all are equally significant and valued in His eyes.

To all of us is issued the equal call and honor of fishing for men in the realm or realms to which we are assigned. To then know our "equipment and tackle," our "waters," and our "fish" falls to us. It falls to Christian grandfathers, fathers, uncles, brothers, and mentors to make the young in their lives into fishers of men—to provide the lessons and experience enabling them to respond to the calling of Jesus that lies at the core of our mandate from Him and our walk with Him.

In preparing the young for the task of becoming effective fishers of men, there is no better way to begin the process of training than to teach them to fish. With the knowledge of the basic concepts and principles of fishing established, the transition of the same into the endeavor of fishing for men becomes a natural and easy one. The time shared together in the solitude of the waters will provide manifold opportunities to teach the other important lessons of life, both those relevant to fishing for men as well as those relating to other matters. The centrality of fishing to the core of the paramount assignment left to us all by Jesus Himself—first inherently in His call to Peter and Andrew, again after the breakfast of roasted fish on the shore of the Sea of Galilee, and finally, with crystal clarity, in the Great Commission—would suggest a reason and a persuasive line of logic for all Christian fathers to consider teaching their sons and daughters the rudiments of fishing.

While numerous principles to be learned through hunting can be applicable to the endeavor of drawing men to the light of the gospel of Christ, it is fishing—more than hunting and to a far greater extent than any other human pursuit—that most parallels the effort to win the souls of men amid the raging battles of evil against good. Thus Jesus did not tell Peter and Andrew that he would make them hunters of men, pursuers of men, teachers of men, preachers to men, or luminaries for men. Rather, He said that He would make them fishers of men.

The waters of the world vary in content, form, and movement. Although a tremendous diversity of fish may be caught, they cannot all be taken in the same way. There are many ways to fish for them—probably more ways than we know.

Many Ways to Fish

As for our experience, we fish primarily with rods and reels of varying styles and sizes depending upon the fish sought. We have fly-fished for trout in the high western streams and lakes with some of the lightest of rods and gone into the deep sea with heavy rods and lines. We have taken fish in the waters of the Mediterranean and the Middle East with only hook and line. In the clear waters of Live Oak Creek in the desert country of western Texas, we have taken large catfish with homemade spears and lantern light by night. At low tide in the darkest hours of night off the shores of Oahu, when the sea stills and the clear water appears as if you are looking through glass, we have waded in with lanterns hanging upon our necks and fished with spears. The Hawaiians call this "torching." In the muddy ponds of southeast Texas we have seined with nets, which can be an exciting way to fish there since we always caught a lot of fish but often also large snapping turtles and the ubiquitous water moccasins, a venomous snake that also is very fast on the water. To say that the sudden appearance of such creatures liven up a fishing trip would be a bit of an understatement. While they move quick and easily in the water, you, being waist-deep or more with your feet submerged in mud, cannot.

My friend Jason, who is closer than a brother and something of a modern west-Texas incarnation of Ishmael, is deadly with bow and arrow. Fishing from the banks or cliffs of the Devil's River in the desert of western Texas, he has taken many massive alligator gar—an incredibly well-armored fish with a fearsome set of sharp teeth that look like a remnant of the dinosaur period and a tiny descendant of a Leviathan ancestor—with his bow. In bow fishing, a line is tied to the back of the arrow so that the fish can be pulled in when hit.

Fishing, Not Hunting, for Men

There are numerous ways to hunt as well. One option open to hunters is an aggressive one. In many kinds of terrain, you can go to where you know or suspect the animals to be and put pressure on them. You can drive them out into the open either on foot or with dogs. If you are good enough, then you can track a single animal for hours, or even for days, until you can get into range for a shot. The hunter can be always moving, always pursuing, and always applying pressure.

The fisherman, though, especially in waters with any significant depth or breadth, has no such option. Aggression, other than merely that of keeping lines in the water or continuing to search the water and sink nets, gains him nothing. You cannot track a bass or drive marlin and tuna into a hook. Even in the most aggressive forms of fishing—that done with bows, spears, or nets, you still are dependent upon the fish being where you expect them to be, for you can do nothing to force them up from the depths or to drive them there from other parts of vast waters. The empty nets of Peter and his companions after a full night of fishing are revelatory of the fact.

Knowing your equipment, the water, and the fish, then, all you can do is to go out, keep lines or nets in the water, and wait. With spears or bow, you can only go, remain ready, and keep looking. Herein, perhaps, is to be found the most revealing parallel between fishing and being fishers of men.

To draw men to the light of the gospel and the saving grace of Jesus Christ, you do not pursue them relentlessly and hunt them down. Rather, you go to the places where you know they should be, go about your business in the proper way, remain diligent and ready, and then keep your lines or nets in the water. Men cannot be—and were not meant to be—hunted down for Christ. We are meant, through deportment, action, and word, to draw them to Christ. In the same way that a good fisherman, with knowledge, diligence, and patience, finds or draws fish, so are all genuine followers of Christ to find and draw men.

Putting Lines into the Water

When going to sea, we prefer the boats in which they set four or five poles and put out as many lines. The more the better. You do not need to be a seasoned fisherman to realize that your chances of getting a strike will rise commensurate with the number of lines put into the water. Too, multiple lines leave open the probability of multiple strikes—one of the most exciting occurrences in fishing when all hands must be on deck, pole in hand, pulling in fish. The spiritual equivalent, of course, is even more fulfilling.

Just as in fishing in waters, when fishing for men, you should concern yourself with only the things that you can control. Study, listen, and observe so as to build knowledge and cultivate wisdom, discernment, and understanding. Be in the place or places that you are supposed to be. Live and fulfill all obligations in accordance with the Word of God. Beyond these actions, all then that you can do—and what you must do according to the call and command of Jesus—is to keep your lines in the water at all times, remaining patient and ready for whatever may strike.

When you live your life in truth and the pursuit of righteousness and justice, you are putting lines into the water. When reaching out to help others in times of sickness, hardship, or need, you put lines into the water. When demonstrating forgiveness, compassion, mercy, or any other of the actions of love, you put your lines into the water. When you answer people's questions about God and Scripture with all honesty, integrity, and courage, regardless of their attitudes or ends, you are putting lines into the water. To proclaim the message of the gospel or to share your own personal faith is to put lines in the water. To act always with physical and moral courage, standing boldly for the principles of truth and righteousness when such are attacked, is to put lines in the water. To walk by faith and to pray is constantly to go out, sinking your net into the water.

Culmination of the Call

When Jesus, Peter, and the other disciples finished their breakfast of roasted fish on the shore of the Sea of Galilee—likely at Tabgha, just over a mile west of Capernaum, a fishermen's suburb frequented by Jesus and His disciples—and lingered around the small fire for a time in conversation and reflection, the presence of friendship and peace among them was confirmed and solidified so as to remain from that point into eternity. With that established, Jesus directed their hearts and minds with His final words toward eternity and the plight of immortal souls. What followed was the culmination of the call to become fishers of men and of all the lessons He had taught them over the past three years to that end.

After glancing up at the massive haul of fish still in the net at the lake's shore, Jesus looked to Peter and asked, "Simon, son of John, do you love Me more than these?"

When Peter answered in the affirmative, Jesus said to him, "Tend My lambs." Jesus then asked the question again, and Peter gave the same answer. Jesus said in reply, "Shepherd My sheep." When Jesus asked the question a third time, Peter was grieved, but he replied with the same answer. Jesus said, "Tend My sheep."

The first step in being an obedient and effective fisher of men is to draw as many as you can unto faith and salvation in Jesus Christ. The second step—and one inherently intertwined with the first—is faithfully and properly to disciple those who do strike your submerged lines and come to Christ or to "tend' them and "shepherd" them in the ways and precepts of our Lord. Just as there is work to be done by a fisherman after bringing back his catch, whether preparing the fish for food or for sale, so, too, is there work to be done by fishers of men for any catch they bring in. Those who respond and call upon Christ must be tended and shepherded so that they, too, become effective fishers of men.

The overriding point that Jesus is making is simply a reiteration of the purpose and course He had set for Peter and Andrew on that same shoreline three years before when He called them to become fishers of men. Jesus was reminding them that He came wholly for spiritual purposes. The battle—and ultimately the war—which He would fight and win was spiritual. The battle to which Peter, Andrew, and all of us who follow in their steps are called is a spiritual one. In that battle, what is ultimately being fought over are the souls of all people. Our command of action in the battle is to try to draw the hearts and minds of as many as we can toward the saving grace of our Lord. Our objective in so doing is to become effective fishers of men.

More Fishing Lessons

Hidden Reefs

A few additional lessons from fishing may be worthy of consideration. All who have taken a boat to sea should know the dangers of hidden reefs. Many ships and boats, great and small, have been ruined or sunk upon colliding with such. Countless lives have been lost as a result. Either carelessness or a failure to know well your vessel and the waters that you will enter can leave you vulnerable to disaster.

Jude, the half-brother of Jesus, warns of "hidden reefs" and the "wild waves of the sea" that crash over them (Jude 12-13). The "hidden reefs" and "wild waves" of which Jude wrote were men who entered the church teaching false doctrines. They were arrogant men who sought to pervert the teachings of Christ to fulfill their own lusts and who flattered others for the sake of gaining advantage for themselves (v. 16). They were men who sought to cause division among the faithful and who acted in worldly ways (v. 19). As an astute fisher of men, you must be aware of the hidden reefs, both for your own sake and for the sakes of those whom you help bring to Christ and then shepherd. You must know what and where the reefs are so as to avoid them or to be able to negotiate the waters close around them. Even the best of fishermen are finished and useless, at least for a time, if their boats are torn apart upon a hidden reef.

Danger Zones of the Sea

When going out on the waters, you will always find dangers inherent but particularly so when going to sea. The sea can be much more unpredictable and tumultuous than are rivers and lakes. Further, many more creatures—in number and variety—are found therein. They can poison you in varying degrees, take bites out of you, or turn you into a meal or a protein snack.

To go into the waters, though, such as when engaging in one of the varied methods of spearfishing, generally will increase the danger around you. If not for the remarkably sharp eyes of the Hawaiians with whom I fished, at least twice I would have stepped on stingrays, submerged and concealed in the sand, while torching. I still marvel at their ability to spot these dangers, but they surely saved me from what would have been a painful gash. On a successful night of torching, as you end up dragging a stringer of dead, bleeding fish in the water behind you, the sharks sometimes move in. As crippling and fatal shark attacks have occurred—and continue to occur in currently rising numbers—in the shallowest of water, torching necessitates that you keep your eyes open and active and your head "on a swivel." If not vigilant, then you are likely to lose some or all of your fish at the least, and you could lose valued parts of your body.

The lesson therein for a fisher of men is the necessity of constant awareness and vigilance in certain waters. For example, if you fish for men in vice-ridden environments where temptations of many kinds abound, then be wary and constantly vigilant with regard both for your own heart and mind as well as for all that is going on around you. In such environments, you may find yourself fishing more from within the water than upon it. Many devoted and well-intentioned men have had their ministries and lives ruined when, letting caution and vigilance falter, they succumbed to the powerful temptations and snares, which for so long had surrounded them.

Predators

Sometimes you get a hard strike, set the hook well, and begin the long process of bringing in a fine fish. You do everything right and all seems to be going well when, suddenly, either far down or out in the sea or right at the boat's edge, a powerful shark strikes and takes the fish off of the line. I once lost a very nice grouper to a much larger and more powerful bull shark in just that way. I had made good progress and all felt fine until the shark struck. The hit was so powerful that I was wholly unable to generate any resistance. In little more than a second or two, the line snapped and the grouper was gone.

Satan and the demonic legions, the spiritual forces of wickedness in the heavenly places, are active at all times and in all places. Some will be drawn to your witness; and though all feels and appears to be right, they will be struck and taken off of your line before they can be "landed." There will be times, as the forces of evil and good battle over wavering human souls, that this is unavoidable. What seems to be secured may be lost.

Sometimes, however, the diligent work of a fisherman in collaboration with others may save a catch that, though well hooked, apparently will be lost to swarming predators. I once had on my line a fine Almaco jack that was about to be taken by a hungry and fast-moving school of porpoises. Though I thought that the fish would be lost, I kept on fighting as hard as I could. While I did all that I could do, the captain threw his boat into reverse and, through some masterful maneuvering on fairly rough seas, backed the porpoises off just long enough for us to pull the fish into the boat. The closest porpoise was only a few yards away, at best, and was coming up fast when we were finally able to lift the fish from the water.

Several lessons may be taken by fishers of men. First, never give up. Never cease fighting with all of the strength, intelligence, and innovation that you can bring. Second, always seek the counsel and help of others whom you trust. Third, that which appears will be lost may still be saved. What you cannot accomplish alone on behalf of another soul—or in any worthy undertaking—may yet be possible when working with others and allowing for the contribution of their knowledge and skills.

False Security

Finally, be wary of presumptions of safety and feelings of invulnerability. Going upon or into the waters are not the only times when a fisherman is at risk. Numerous African rivers afford tremendous fishing opportunities. Some, such as the Zambezi, are beautiful, their shores imparting a feeling of serenity and security—at least to those not thoroughly familiar with all that swims or walks within them. Many people, and some fishermen, have been quickly taken and never seen again while standing on dry land. Others have been crushed to death by hippos who simply objected to any creature of significant size coming between them and the sanctuary of their water. Hippos, too, have been known to attack fishing boats and canoes, taking massive bites out of both the vessels and the fishermen therein.

In the spiritual battles of life, there will be dangers where you expect and know them to be. Yet what appears to be serene or secure may not necessarily be so. Thus the daily walk with God and the endeavor to fish for men is best not undertaken without unceasing prayer and constant vigilance.

All who would follow Christ must then take up the charges to become fishers of men and to train up others to do the same. Where you live, in which circles you move, and the kind and number of people you draw matters not. All that matters is that, ever faithfully, you fish.

CHAPTER 11

WHAT TO DO ON AN EXPEDITION WITH A BOY

Given the fact that the vast majority of young men eagerly anticipate a journey to hunt, fish, or just comb the wilderness, there is little a father can do that will have more long-term impact on the life of the child. As a matter of fact, many hunters have found that even daughters love this experience with Dad, and indeed sometimes the whole family can go along.

Every little boy in America needs a father, but the tragedy unfurled for the world to see was made known by the Dartmouth University Medical School in a nationwide survey called "Hardwired to Connect." In an effort to determine the cause of increasing gang-related crime in the large cities of America, Dartmouth made every effort to ascertain the nature of the cause and admitted considerable surprise with the answer they found—the absent father. Any fair assessment of this problem in America today links gang-related crime, serious illegal drug use, abuse of alcoholic beverages, teen pregnancy, the birth of thousands of children with no responsible father, and, most desperate of all, suicide, directly to the fact that one in every two little boys growing up in America does not have a father figure living in the home.

What makes this particularly tragic is the fact that it is so easily remedied. Not only can fathers be placed back in positions of importance, having been undermined by *Roe v. Wade* and the absurd conclusion that only the woman has a say in whether or not the child lives; but also, people can acknowledge the desperation of children, even little girls, growing up in a home without a father and acknowledge that there are numerous ways by which this problem could be remedied.

One such way is paternal surrogacy—that is, taking a little boy in your community who is not your own but has no father and becoming a father figure to him. This has been one of the greatest joys of my own life, personally, and I warmly commend it to all.

But what exactly is a man to do with his boy in an outdoor outing? Consider the following ten responsibilities. Although they are not given in order of importance, each of them is important and suggests a beginning point for any father.

(1) Give the boy the very best chance possible to take game, but do not make it a perfect situation where he will know no disappointments. Jerry Davenport, a dear friend mentioned earlier, had a modest 12,000-acre ranch in west Texas. He was kind enough to ask us to come out and hunt. Taking my son Armour for the first time when he was just nine years of age, we bounced across the rough terrain of his ranch in the jeep. The very first day I watched as Armour took a nice 8-point buck with an incredibly long shot. Now he thought this was easy and "no problem." About the third day out, in a flat area, a huge buck greeted the jeep by suddenly jumping to his feet. Since we never got close enough to be sure, we could not tell for certain, but it appeared that he was at least a 12-point buck, which would have scored very high. The base of his horns looked like cedar trees. Armour, who has always been quick to shoot and fundamentally quite accurate, blazed away, having leaped from the jeep. Down went the deer with an unbelievable shot. We were all amazed, although Armour tried to act as though it was just normal. But he made one fatal mistake. He did not chamber another round. We still do not know for sure what happened, but we suspect that Armour's .30-06 bullet made solid contact right at the base of the horns and rolled the big buck, probably knocking him out. However, since he went down so hard and we did not immediately approach and Armour did not have another bullet chambered, as he did approach the fallen animal, suddenly the buck jumped up and ran off. What a prize totally lost and apparently virtually unharmed. Well it was a great lesson to learn. Armour had learned both the joy of taking game and the sorrows of making a mistake. These are the kinds of situations that we need to create. Take a boy where he can fish but preferably not somewhere where they're jumping into the boat with him. He needs to learn both hardship and ecstasy.

(2) **Toughen your son with exposure to the elements and terrain.** My son and son-in-law have now hunted with me in Africa as well as in the tough country of west Texas and elsewhere. They have known what it means to trudge on when the thermometer is at 22° and a north wind, like tiger teeth, is tearing at their clothes. They have shivered around a campfire, desperately trying to warm up cold limbs, and they have known what it means to climb mountains, descend to the valleys, climb mountains again, and so forth—all in search of one wounded animal. As a result, they have learned what it means to face almost invincible odds and prevail. There is no lesson in life that could be any more important than this lesson, and it can be taught nowhere quite as well as on a hunt.

(3) **Introduce your son to other good hunters and their practices.** When I first began hunting Africa, I suppose I had fairly good intuitions, but the truth of the matter is that I knew almost nothing about hunting in a significant way. I had just never had the opportunity. In fact, I was in my early forties before the opportunity came to me. I cannot begin to tell you how grateful I am to a group that probably now exceeds 40

or 50 men who have invested in the lives of my son and son-in-law. I do not feel threatened by these men at all, and I am so grateful that they took time to instruct my boys in firearms and their use, as well as hunting methods and understandings. Not only am I grateful to these men in America and to professional hunters in Africa, but I am also forever grateful for the exposure that my boys had to African trackers.

These trackers are incredible individuals. With very little formal education, they have mastered their world. They know the animals and their ways. On one occasion, when Armour had hit a steenbok, we could not find it anywhere. A group of trackers, about 12 in number, got into a vivid and quite vociferous discussion about the whole issue. They were arguing over a particular place where hundreds of animals had walked through the dirt. I could see them pointing and hear their animation, and I was very fearful that intertribal warfare might break out at any moment. The chief instrument they were using to point to various things was a machete. This went on for about 35 minutes, at which point they calmed down. They all turned, and the spokesman announced, "We will find Armour's animal 400 yards immediately southwest of us, and it is hit in the rear left leg." My first thought was, "Yes, sure. I'm also going to be the head mother at the local convent beginning next month." But sure enough, we found the animal exactly where they said we would find him, and he was hit exactly where they said he was hit. How they knew I do not know. But I am forever grateful that my sons have enjoyed the teaching moments from these men. Today, both of my sons know more about hunting, more about animals, more about the use of firearms than I do—because of the multitude of their teachers.

(4) Take your children fishing often. I stress this not only because of the chapters in this book on fishing, but because hunting is normally limited to a certain time of the year. For example, some animals can be taken year-round and without license in Texas, but for the most part, all of that is regulated as it should be. Fishing, however, in some way or another, is pretty well a year-round possibility, so plan to take your son fishing. So many lessons can be taught through fishing, as has been indicated in the breadth of the book.

(5) Use the silent times on the hunt or a fishing trip to reach out to God and to teach your sons about Him. Church is important, and your son needs to have the experience of corporate worship with all ages and both men and women present. That said, I can promise you he will learn truths about God from a godly father and grandfather while he is on the hunt far beyond what he has learned in Sunday School. First, there are few distractions. Second, he is being treated as a man and not as a boy, and he will warm to that immediately. Third, you can talk about things forever without the bell ringing and the conversation coming to a conclusion. You can talk about what it means to protect the rights of the weak in society and give them a chance also. You can talk about the nature of God and His love for us. You can talk about how to be "fishers of men." All of it can be done on the hunting or fishing trip in a way that cannot be duplicated.

(6) Let your son observe how you handle your own mistakes and disappointments. While seeing you rejoice and succeed is important for your son, to see your mistakes and your disappointments is just as important. He will have many disappointments in life. Life is not fair, and sin has taken a terrible toll on the social order. People are inevitably going to mistreat him. As a result of all these things, some turn to drugs or alcohol. A tragically large number, growing by the day, are turning to suicide. If your son sees that you use the disappointments of life as stepping stones to spiritual greatness and trust in the providence of God, he will learn that he can do that also. If he learns this, he has grasped a lesson more important than any lesson he could possibly learn about hunting or fishing. Dad, don't fail him at this point.

(7) Make your son conserve and prepare the game or fish that he has taken. I have succeeded pretty well with my son and son-in-law in helping them to conserve the game they have taken—carefully field dressing and preparing the hide and head for display. Unfortunately, I never really learned the culinary arts myself, so I must confess that the ultimate preparation of the game for eating has not been my prowess. Thankfully, my son Armour did not let that keep him from learning. Beginning with his careful observation of our African cooks, he has learned to do more than the well-trained chef can do with most of the game and fish that he prepares. This skill, too, will make him a better hunter and a better fisherman.

(8) Teach your son how to make camp, how to clean up after the camp is broken, and how to cook over the campfire and in the dirt. All of this, of course, is not easy, and it amounts to work, but that is its great virtue. There are kinds of work that are essentially boring, and children assigned to do those jobs struggle with them and develop wrong attitudes toward diligent labor. But a boy who has responsibility first of making camp, putting up the tents, arranging the sleeping bags, building the fire, and then, upon departure, cleaning up the countryside so that there is virtually no indication that a camper was even in the vicinity, while hard, will be work that he will learn to enjoy. As he enjoys doing hard work, he is being prepared for all of life.

(9) Always pray first and last on any expedition. Before leaving, ask that if it can be within God's will He will give you success but that most of all He will watch over you and give you safety. This opportunity can be used to impress upon your son the fact that there is danger in the field and in the presence of weapons. Make them especially wary of the often fatal mix of firearms with alcohol and/or drugs while being out with other men in the field. Thus, he needs to take care, but he also should ask for the intervention of God. Upon returning from the hunt or the fishing trip, there is the opportunity to express gratitude to

God for the safety that He has given and also to give gratitude to God for the game or fish that has been made available. This way your son learns to pray about things that matter, and he learns the benefit and the power of prayer. "The effective, fervent prayer of a righteous man avails much" (James 5:16b, NKJV).

(10) Teach him to respect all of the animals and, more important still, to love and care for his mother, sisters, and little brothers. If he learns to respect and honor the animals that God has made in the world, he can easily transfer that to a deeper respect for his family. From that you can teach him to love his mother unconditionally and to love his sisters and little brothers and care for them. In fact, sibling rivalries will tend not to occur as often when your "man" has been taught that he has responsibility for their well-being. In those times when you are absent, which, in my case, were way too many, he knows that he is in charge of the safety of the home. My son knew that by the time he was six years old. Admittedly, he might not have been able to do much about it at that point in time; yet he felt responsible. As a result, it has made him a man greatly loved by all who come in contact with him—simply because they know that he will accept responsibility for every one of them should they need help in any way.

Armed with these ten understandings, a man is ready for the field. While it is true that you may need to learn some skills to go with it, and many of you may need to learn to use a firearm or a bow, the most important thing is that you are out there. You do not have to be a pro. All you need to be is a willing father and grandfather—willing to undergo the difficulties involved in getting your sons and grandsons outdoors. This effort is something that God will bless, and it may just be the greatest need in America today.

CHAPTER 12

WHY BOYS NEED A FATHER

In beginning this chapter, let me say that this is no denigration of the value of Mom. First of all, none of us would be here if it were not for Mom. If there are no other reasons to be grateful to our mothers, that fact would be a good place to begin. However, mothers make incredible contributions to young men as well as to young women. Those contributions are somewhat different, although some factors are the same for both genders. Most of the attitudes that develop in small children are developed initially by the mother. Of course, anyone who has an idea about life knows that attitudes—i.e., how a person views life and the others who cross his path in life—will determine how effective he is and how well he does. So Mom, for any number of reasons, is absolutely indispensable. As a matter of fact, God intended for each child to have a mother and a dad, and that's precisely the reason it works biologically, to say nothing of psychologically and spiritually. Mom is important.

On the other hand, Dad is absolutely crucial, especially for the development of boys. There is a sixth sense about manhood. Little girls, from earliest moments of their lives, become interested in dolls, clothes, and numerous other naturally feminine pursuits. Little boys seldom do that. Quite to the contrary, most little boys could care less about how they're dressed and find getting dressed up to be a painful and useless experience endured mostly for the sake of Mom. They are intuitively interested in critters, can't wait until they are given a dog, and love to do things outdoors, including wrestling with other kids from the neighborhood. Speaking of dogs, by the way, any parent who is in a position to do so needs to be sure that Junior has a big dog—a dog he can be proud of and that shakes the whole house when it barks. Believe me, a dog makes a difference in the development of his manhood. That sixth sense of manhood can only be augmented by a father whom he sees and honors. In another chapter, I have mentioned the study from Dartmouth Medical School titled "Hardwired to Connect." One of the amazing results that arose from that study was the discovery that even when Dad is a bum, even when he is abusive and a terror to his home, and even though little boys may fear him and run from him, yet they admire him profoundly. When they grow up, they want to be just like Dad. Therein is the tragedy of abusive behavior.

In fact, in my hunters' banquets, I never cease to remind those hunters that whether they go to heaven or hell is a choice they make. But the tragedy of the choice to go to hell is not just their own loss but the probable loss of their whole family. Churches will make every effort to win their families to Christ, but all the statistics say exactly the same thing. When the husband comes to Christ, eventually the whole family will come to Christ. If, on the other hand, the mother alone comes to Christ, as the years go by the children will drift away. As I say in those banquets I say here also: Dad, if you're not a believer, as you fall over the precipice into hell, look behind you. Your boy may be 13, 33, or 53, but he'll probably be following. You can take your son to hell, or you can come to Christ yourself and take your whole family with you to heaven.

Given the sixth sense of manhood that is in a boy, there are certain things that, really, only Dad can do. First of all, only you, Dad, can give your child a sense of the value of tackling a physical challenge. If he learns to attempt great physical challenges, then those he faces in other areas of life will not overcome him but will be steps to victory. Second, if a boy grows up observing his father exhibiting both love and forgiveness, then he will learn those two most important aspects of life. Love is not defined here in the syrupy, sentimental ways that the world sees it, but rather as the New Testament defines it. Love is totally focused on other people. Love does not ask, "How can I use you for my benefit? How can I exploit your advantages?" but rather, "What can I do to make your life better?"

Forgiveness is a divine art. Nobody does this one like God does, as He exhibits in the forgiveness that Christ poured out while on the cross. Praying for those who were in the process of nailing Him to the tree, He said, "Father, forgive them; for they do not know what they are doing" (Luke 23:34). Then to a lonely figure being crucified along with Him, who simply asked to be remembered by Jesus in His kingdom, Jesus said, "Today you shall be with Me in Paradise" (Luke 23:43), apparently forgiving the man's sin. Jesus is the greatest example of forgiveness who ever lived, but the one who will teach your boy about forgiveness must be you, Dad, and you, Granddad. They must see this modeled through you, and then they will understand it in the Lord and practice it themselves.

Next, seeing Dad and Granddad being obedient to God's law and to man's law will make an incredible difference in their lives. There may come a time when, of course, a man must be disobedient to man's law in order to be obedient to God's law. That distinction is one that will also not be lost on your son as he observes your behavior. Nevertheless, man's law is actually God's law, according to the New Testament (Romans 13:1-7), but God's prescribed law in the Bible is not a listing of "dos and don'ts." Rather, God's law is an outline of how people are to live in order to be deeply satisfied, wonderfully content, and overwhelmingly productive in life. All of this can be promised your son if he will follow your obedience to God's law and to man's law.

Another reason a boy needs a dad is to teach him the gifts of working and creating with both body and mind. I wish that I had discovered this principle early enough to teach my son auto mechanics. Unfortunately, I grew up in an era when automobile mechanics was considered something to which the kids who not very smart in school gave themselves. What a tragedy! How much money would I have saved for my family across the years if I could have done some simple things, like changing the oil, in my automobile? If I had developed greater physical skills, I would have accomplished in my children a work ethic that would have both saved money and been wonderfully productive in other ways.

Still another reason why a boy needs a father is to learn to love the Word of God and to love attaining a variety of knowledge in every area. Of course, this means that the father and grandfather have to develop these capacities themselves, but that is one of the great joys of having a son. You and your son can develop these abilities together. Mom can make a contribution to the love of the Word of God. But once again, Dad is the decisive one. If Dad is a man who speaks often of the Word of God and who is regularly observed by his son reading the Bible and if he applies its truths skillfully to all of life as we have tried to do in the pages of this book, you can imagine the effect of that upon the child.

Dads need to be present in the lives of their sons to show them how to respond to both difficulty and danger. Life is difficult and not infrequently is dangerous. Despite many sons who cower before the difficulty and the danger, there are some who inevitably demonstrate courage. This development of courage is seldom done in isolation from the father. Please understand that we do not speak here of bravado. Bravado is the boastful type of courage that often folds up under pressure. Here we are speaking of genuine courage—the ability to stand alone when necessary and the ability to do the right thing no matter what the danger involved. A son watches a father very closely and will learn that lesson early if it is taught.

In the Hebrew synagogues, a boy was considered to be a man at age twelve. At the time he went through his *bar-mitzvah*, he became a "son of the law." Now we all know that at age twelve there is still a great deal of boy left in him, and he is only beginning to sense his blossoming manhood. But that is exactly the moment at which he needs to be told, "You're a man." There is no adolescence in the Bible. That has been skillfully pointed out by several biblical commentators, but little attention has been paid to it by a social order that, generally speaking, wishes to excuse whatever bad behavior may exist in teenagers. The Bible knows only boyhood and manhood and that change takes place at the age of twelve. This concept is one that we need to pass on to our children, and nobody can do that as effectively as the father.

The father will teach the use of firearms, blades, and hands in self-protection. A child who grows up with a godly father and learns the use of firearms, knives, and hands in protection of the weak is not the child you ever have to worry about doing something harmful. However, he is a child of whom you are going to be proud all his life because he will know how to use all of those effectively and for good.

Today, I am an old man, but the truth is that even in my youth I did not enjoy the physical strength or defense capabilities of my son and son-in-love. And I am grateful that on only two occasions in adult life have I had to fight, the last as a 69-year-old man. Only once have I had to draw a firearm. But how grateful I am that my sons know they have a dad who will take that risk even now if necessary to protect their mother and others who are not strong. In turn, I have no doubt in the world what either of them will do. A boy needs to see his daddy pray and hear him read God's Word. There is no substitute for knowing that Dad loves God and finds God's Word to be a matter of major consequence. To hear Dad talking to God in prayer proves to a son that such a practice is strength and not weakness. He will come to see the practice as spiritual weight training.

A dad is needed in a boy's life to teach him to laugh. When the little boy falls and scratches himself, he tends to get up crying. For a few moments, he indeed should be comforted. But before long, the whole incident needs to be treated as one of laughter. Whenever Dad hits his thumb with the hammer, the same needs to be true. If Dad laughs hysterically at the bad things that happen in life, the son will learn to laugh also, and that laughter will see him through many sorrows.

Finally, take your son to see as much of God's world as you possibly can. My father did that for me, and, in turn, I have done it for my children. A family has only so much money, but families who waste that money with ever larger electronic means and leave their children ignorant of the cultures and landscapes of the world have done them a major disfavor. Seeing the world in the presence of the dad, noting his curiosity about it and learning to have that same curiosity will make them world citizens. My kids—now all grownups—are anything but perfect. But one thing is true: They are comfortable wherever they are tonight in the world. They have learned to love God's world and to see it as the place and the people that He created. I pray that they have learned that well from their dad and hence have a lively curiosity about the whole of life.

CHAPTER 13

A CHURCH FOR MEN IS A CHURCH FOR ALL

Numerous monographs lamenting the feminization of the church have appeared in recent years. Some of these have been better than others, but to date there are few that outline exactly how one would go about the process of putting together a church for men. Cowboy churches and country churches have demonstrated the truths of the dictum that if you win the husband/father you will eventually reach the entire family for Christ. The following suggestions are not exhaustive, but they offer insights into ways by which masculine-friendly churches can be developed.

Reaching the entire family for Christ is our primary concern. Our thesis is simply stated above: Reach the husband/father, and in the majority of cases you will also reach the wife and children. On the other hand, reaching the wife or the children, both critically important endeavors, clearly does not guarantee that the husband/father will follow, though in some cases he will. Furthermore, this is not to denigrate the importance of the church's ministry to the unmarried, to widows, and to single parents with children. All of this outreach is more important than ever before. But while there are programs and approaches available and while most of our churches are in tune with this need, few churches have reflected deeply on the need for reaching the head of the household, the husband. So with our congratulations, encouragement, and enthusiastic support for every church that has a program for reaching any segment of the social order, we nevertheless put forward a program that will win men and keep boys in the church.

Sadly, young people, especially older teenage boys, tend to abandon the church as soon as they are able to do so. A part of this problem is generated from the failure of the church to do all that it can to assure the genuineness of conversion. A youth who experiences godly sorrow for his sin, leading to repentance and salvation, may certainly stray for a period of time; but the very fact of his experience with Christ will bring him back to the church, for which the Bible says the Lord loved and gave Himself. But the problem that exists is magnified by "easy believism" and the tendency to baptize young people before they are capable of making an informed, adult decision to follow Christ. The failure extends to poor instruction at the time of baptism and the failure to make clear that baptism is a covenant with Christ determining what kind of life will be lived. So with all this in mind, consider twenty options available to create a church that will win men and keep men and boys in the church.

(1) In preaching and teaching, pay careful attention to passages that magnify masculine character traits and strengths. In the volume that you have just read, you have observed an emphasis on multiple passages of Scripture about which few sermons or lessons are ever delivered. Most of the people doing the preaching and teaching have not or cannot really identify with the experiences outlined in these passages of Scripture because their lives are part of a totally different culture. But good hermeneutics (the science of biblical interpretation) demands that the preacher or teacher do his homework and be able to assist the student learner in crossing the divide of cultures. Choosing to preach on those texts or use them illustratively in the process of the sermon or lesson provides an atmosphere in which most men and boys will feel at home. With such an approach, young men will not be as likely to heed the call to identify with radical Islam and the hatred that it breeds.

(2) Give men a mission challenge that involves them in a difficult and nearly impossible endeavor. Men like a challenge. The higher the mountain to climb and the more difficult the circumstances surrounding that climb, the more they are apt to undertake such an endeavor. There are certainly adroit female mountain climbers, but the vast majority who attempt such feats are still male, a situation that is not likely to change in the near future.

Several years ago Tom Elliff, who was serving at that time as president of the International Mission Board of the Southern Baptist Convention, asked me if Southwestern Baptist Theological Seminary, where I serve, would be willing to take the gospel to an unreached people group. I immediately replied, "No, under no circumstances." Elliff was clearly a little bit taken back and managed to ask why. I replied, "Because you will not give me what I want." Curious, he replied, "What do you want?" And I replied, "In order to get my students to undertake such a mission, it has to be almost impossible. I want an unreached people group somewhere so remote in the world that it is a major difficulty just to get to the people, a people group among whom, in so far as we know, there has been no receptivity to the gospel. Furthermore, I want it to be a large number of people." Elliff said, "I will get back to you in a few days."

Triumphantly Elliff called back a few days later and said, "Well I have your group. I want you to take the Antandroy people group in southern Madagascar. The rains and the muddy roads make it virtually impossible to get there most of the year. As far as we know, there are no believers in the group, and the region is dangerous territory." Well, I studied a bit about the Antandroy people and discovered that there were more than a million of them and that they were called "the people of the thorn," giving an indication of the difficulty of access to them. But our Lord wore a crown of thorns when He died on the cross, and I could immediately see that the Savior who wore the crown of thorns wore it for the people of the thorn.

Going to our students I explained to them who these people were, where they were located, the near impossibility of getting to them, and the fact that there would be unique dangers to them personally—physically, mentally, and spiritually. Completing my explanation in chapel with more than a thousand students present I said, "How many of you, health permitting, are willing to go to the Antandroy people in southern Madagascar?" Now I had a new problem. I am not sure that every student lifted his hand, but there were so many hands in the air that I could see nothing but a sea of hands as students immediately responded. Foremost among them were our male students who immediately saw the challenge as one that they would like to undertake.

When you give men a challenge that will require spiritual, mental, and physical preparation, they will respond to it on almost every occasion. Never hesitate to provide those kinds of challenges. Some will even arise from men themselves, but a church that challenges its men to do the difficult and the nearly impossible will never have a problem getting men into church.

(3) Limit the number of soft songs about syrupy sentimentalism, which, for the most part, have little appeal to men. However, this is not to say that men will not sing. When men know the song and when the lyrics extol manly endeavors anointed by the Spirit of the living God, they will surely respond.

Standing one day by a 14-year-old boy, I asked, "Why do you guys stand for every song? I am an old man and by the time I stand for the entire song service and then have to stand to preach, I'm tired." He looked at me with some puzzlement and then said, "Well, you have to do something. You can't sing the songs." I understood exactly what he meant. This is not a criticism of all contemporary music. We must never forget that once upon a time "The Old Rugged Cross" was a contemporary song. Contemporary simply means recently written, and it would be a tragedy for Christian hymnody to enter into an era when no new music is produced. However, there are songs that do emphasize masculine traits of God, and those need to be both written anew and recovered from the bin where many have been neatly stored away in response to the effeminate culture.

Let me take one example. Sabine Baring-Gould's famous hymn "Onward Christian Soldiers" has long since been relegated to the Christian closet. Obviously it offended the increasingly acculturated taste of those who never wanted to hear a war theme in church. But, of course, the fact is that the Bible is full of stories about conflict and about war. War is terrible, as anyone who has ever been in a battle will testify. But, unfortunately, it is an abiding testimony to the sinfulness of the race, and there are times, as Augustine well said, when a "just war" is necessary. Valiant and strong men are needed for such a conflict.

When one looks at the lyrics of Onward Christian Soldiers there is not a single thing about physical warfare, but the hymn takes note of the reality of spiritual warfare, and of the weapons that must be employed in order to triumph against Satan successfully. Consider the following words:

> Onward, Christian soldiers, marching as to war,
> With the cross of Jesus going on before!
> Christ, the royal Master, leads again the foe;
> Forward into battle, see his banner go!

> Onward, Christian soldiers, marching as to war,
> With the cross of Jesus going on before!
>
> At the sign of triumph Satan's host doth flee;
> On, then, Christian soldiers, on to victory!
> Hell's foundations quiver at the shout of praise;
> Brothers, lift your voices, loud your anthems raise!
>
> Like a mighty army moves the church of God;
> Brothers, we are treading where the saints have trod;
> We are not divided; all one body we,
> One in hope and doctrine, one in charity.
>
> Onward, then, ye people, join our happy throng,
> Blend with ours your voices in the triumph song;
> Glory, laud, and honor, unto Christ the King;
> This thro' countless ages men and angels sing.

When I was a child, I can well remember seeing men who normally didn't sing belting forth this song when they would sing little else. They identified with the fact and necessity of real men in conflict with the devil and his efforts to expunge Christ from the lives of all men. My point is simply to urge you to watch the lyrics of the songs you sing; and while all of us understand the value of some songs that may not appeal as much to men, a church that wants to reach men will find those hymns and songs that do appeal to men and will use them also.

(4) Place men in instructive positions over boys when the boys reach the age of nine, and hopefully from even earlier; and while you are at it, be careful which men you choose. Some years ago while I was pastor at First Baptist Church in Fayetteville, Arkansas, I approached Dr. Oxford, the vice president at the University of Arkansas, about

A Church for Men Is a Church for All

the possibility of assuming the teaching role for our college students. To my surprise, he said, "Absolutely not." I thought he was refusing to teach, which was strange, because he was a very gifted leader and a very strong Christian. So I said, "What do you want to do this coming year in the church?" He replied to my further astonishment, "I want to work in the nursery." Now I thought that the vice president had lost his way, and so I inquired as to why he wanted to do that. He said, "Don't worry about why. Just give me the assignment. I want to be there to take the babies from the arms of their mothers on their way to Bible study, and you will see what will happen." He was exactly right. The mothers lined up in a long line to have the privilege of handing their baby to the vice president of the University of Arkansas. He passed the baby on to the ladies who really knew how to care for them, but just the fact that the vice president was there enjoying the baby, encouraging the mother and assuring her that the baby would receive the best care made all the difference in the world. Then I wondered, why didn't I think of that?

One of the biggest mistakes made in trying to reach and keep young men in the church is to give them a female teacher. The problem here is not that the female teacher has nothing of value for them to learn. Quite to the contrary, she has an enormous wealth of information and experience to impart to these young men. My point is not her inability. My point is rather that if we want to keep the young men, then we need to put strong, masculine leadership in front of them from their earliest days. My personal preference would be that there never be a time when the church did not provide a man as a leader for boys in Bible study. But certainly by the time they are nine and beginning to develop their concept of manhood there is great need to see that their leaders are men who not only provide instruction but also model what biblical manhood is all about. Do this one thing and just a few years later you will have plenty of 18, 19, and 20-year-old men in your church.

(5) Have a program to train boys in outdoor life, missions, and Scripture memory. We have mentioned this in an earlier chapter. The old Royal Ambassador program provided just such emphases. Memorizing Scripture, involving the boys in mission outreach, as well as in outdoor life and instruction, were part of the Royal Ambassador program. Other organizations may come close, but there simply is no program that is widely known to be doing this. The fact is that the local church is going to develop such a program and it needs to be the three-legged stool, about which I have spoken, emphasizing all three of these aspects.

(6) When your church is thinking about a welcome center, put together one that at least in part has boys and men in focus. Mix together Bible study, hunting, fishing, and camping. Imagine a man getting out of an automobile and walking into a welcome center at a church. The first thing that he sees is a fly fishing display with a smiling man asking the question, "Have you ever been fly fishing?" Now most men have not been fly fishing, but the very thought of it is appealing to them. So they go over to the table and the man who welcomes them begins to explain how exactly fly fishing provides some of the most exciting moments of a man's life. In the process, he also points the man to a Bible class and has someone to take him down to the Bible class. There the emphasis continues, but the majority of the time is spent in explaining what the Bible means. I can practically guarantee that man will be back.

Imagine a man coming into a welcome center with trophies of deer or other animals on the wall. The smiling welcoming committee says, "Welcome to our church. We recognize that hunting is present on the pages of God's Word. We want to help you with both, and we are happy to have you here. Such an approach is attempted at very few churches to my knowledge, but it would revolutionize the number of men who would come.

(7) In your church, develop programs that emphasize trap shooting, gymnastics, archery, riding, scuba diving qualifications, and things of that nature. Not every church can do every one of these, but almost every church could do some of them. Taking a young man directly from Bible study out back where you teach him archery will guarantee that he wants to do more Bible study extenuated with a little archery. Some will have access to horses. Most men have never ridden but are fascinated by the shear strength and beauty of the muscular horse, and they would be delighted to have the opportunity, especially when they are boys, to learn the fine art of sitting in the saddle. That added to the Bible study will make both a joy and will bring the young man back.

(8) Every man should be challenged with the possibility of embracing a surrogate son. This proposal will be the most difficult of all, but we now know, as indicated earlier, that one out of every two little boys born in the United States does not have a father in the home. Yet, even the most secular of studies has admitted that having a father is critically important to the proper development of young men. Consequently, the most spiritually minded and manly among your congregation ought to be urged to adopt a boy who has no father and see that he gets the instruction needed in whatever is of interest to him and also an understanding of the truths of the Bible and the work of the Savior.

(9) Programs that introduce a young man to some of the basics of life can be taught in the local church. Many of them will not only find interest in these but also will find permanent careers in them. For example, why not have a godly taxidermist teach the basics of taxidermy? This is a great opportunity for artistic expression as well as earning a life's income. When the modern-day hunter takes his animal to the taxidermist, the one thing he knows is that if he is the most fortunate man on earth he will see his animal back and prepared for mounting in nine months, but it will probably be a year—and it might be fifteen months. There are too few taxidermists to handle the load. Why not teach a young man taxidermy as an art form? How about auto mechanics? Then there is the possibility of animal husbandry. For years FFA was prominent in almost all of the smaller high schools in Texas, and hundreds of young men profited by learning animal husbandry. Tremendous opportunities await those who develop expertise in the handling of animals. Many will go on to become veterinarians, for example, and everybody knows that there is a family economy available for veterinarians. Construction, investment financing, and important instruction in charitable giving all ought to take place for the young men taught by godly Christian leaders.

(10) Teach men the proper care and respect for women and children. Each of us is aware of the constant cry of abuse—a cry that should be heard very carefully. The answer to the problem of abuse, however, is not essentially sociological, whether we are talking about physiological assistance or intervention by legal authorities. The primary way to avoid abuse is for godly men who understand the issue carefully to instruct boys at a very early age in how women and children are to be profoundly respected and cared for and never under any circumstances to be abused. When the heart of the young man develops a passion for the things of God and he has been taught to respect women and children appropriately, he will render such service as unto God, and the number of cases of this abuse will experience a definite drop in the social order.

(11) Focus on the geography of the world with its unique peoples and cultures. I do not know many men who are not fascinated by cartography. Most do not know a whole lot about it, but take a man and put him in an art gallery and he will look at the pictures as he passes by, but, with little understanding, he comes to a map of the world and you will not be able to get him to move on. He is fascinated with how the continents developed, who lives on those continents, what kind of animal life is there, etc. So focus on the geography of the world and its unique people and cultures, and you will have the attention of most men.

(12) Offer study times for boys punctuated by outdoor challenges and magnify the acquisition of knowledge. Perhaps you are unaware of the fact of what is happening in the colleges and universities of the country. We now have far more young women than men studying in the colleges and universities. I am thrilled for young women to study in the colleges and the universities, but I am profoundly apprehensive about the number of young men who are opting not to pursue that course when the leaders of the world will almost inevitably be drawn from among those who have availed themselves of a college education. How in the world can this be reversed? The church plays a major role if it will develop study times for men and boys in which they are tutored in that with which they are struggling. They can furthermore be guided to materials that will help them understand the disciplines that arise out of the natural world with outdoor challenges, which can be used effectively to magnify the acquisition of knowledge. Young men will respond to such an emphasis and will do better in their academic work, and many more will go on to college and university.

(13) Be sure that every man has a ministry. Connect the men with disaster relief organizations of which your church may be a part. So often when disasters occur anywhere in the world the disaster relief segment of Southern Baptist life is either first or second to arrive, often beating the Red Cross and remaining available as long as help is needed. Men will respond to such challenges and should be given that opportunity.

(14) Be sure that major leaders are manly men. Never put women leading men. This statement is controversial. It is against all that the modern culture teaches. But it should not be controversial because the

Bible clearly states that women are not to teach men or to rule over men. When you put a woman leading men there will be some among the faithful who will follow no matter what, but the average man on the street will not come back to church and follow feminine leadership. So if you want to reach men, be sure that all the overall leaders of the church are men who have respectability among other men, and do not put a woman in leadership over men. Have women devote their energies to leading women as the New Testament directs (Titus 2:3-5).

(15) Remember that joining hands across the aisle and singing a warm fuzzy chorus is not encouraging to a visiting male but rather is a turn off par excellence. A man simply does not come away from an experience of holding hands with a man he has never met and feel good about the whole experience. Think through your whole church service and be sure you are not asking men to do those things that run contrary to their natural responses. Things may be done from church to church that seem insignificant on the surface but are actually turn-offs for men. Think through it carefully and then proceed.

(16) Pray for significant objects that vitally affect the lives of all but leading a man to see and appreciate the joy of experiencing answers to prayer. Prayers for the conversion of specific lost friends are always in order. When a church begins to pray for the salvation of a given individual, even though it may take months or even years before it happens, a man is able to see God at work and experience an answer to his prayer. It is proper to pray about everything, but too often our prayers are rather selfish, perhaps centering only on physical healing for illnesses or other personal issues. Every need is important to God, but get the men involved in prayer beyond immediate personal requests to set their eyes and hearts on significant objects such as missions sites and the souls of lost men. Men will respond.

(17) Discuss openly, frankly, and appropriately matters of family, sexual intimacy, work place challenges, etc. Most men become very weary of folks who beat around the bush. Trying to be politically correct is something with which a man lives every day in the social order, but he never likes it. He is looking for somebody to discuss things openly, frankly, and appropriately. *Openly* means that we do not hide from any of the facts of life. *Frankly* means we discuss it without hesitation but *appropriately*, especially in matters of family and sexual intimacy, suggests that we do so in the highest moral terms but nevertheless frankly and openly. A man will attend, for example, a discussion of how sexual intimacy is actually supposed to work in the plan of God, and he will profit and come back again.

(18) Involve men in ministry to teens, prostitutes, addicts, inmates at penal facilities, recently-released criminals, etc. The point here is to find a ministry for every man. There are men in every church who can do these kinds of things but who have never considered the possibility. Part of the pastor's responsibility ought to be to discover those ministry opportunities and see to it that the men are initiated into participation in those opportunities. Finding the neediest people in life such as, for example, drug addicts and alcoholics and teaching the men to minister effectively to them is a sure opportunity to keep men involved in the church.

(19) Keep your services lively but not worldly, using men to direct the singing and often to sing. If we give men the idea that singing is what the women do, then they will be turned off. If they see men singing, however, and especially observe that men are directing the program of music in the church, then they will respond. By the same token, services need to be lively—never a funeral dirge. Many a man has come to a dirge at a local church and has walked away saying, "Well, church may be fine for some but it is not for me." Don't give them that opportunity. Make it lively but don't make it worldly. Even a worldly man is able to distinguish between what is godly and what is worldly, and he will not respond to the same thing in church that he sees in the social order.

(20) Teach all your men to preach, teach, and pray publicly. Have them assist you in funerals and weddings. I know that such an encouragement is strange to the ears of many, but when your men begin to conceive of themselves as ministers of the gospel and not simply hearers of the Word, they will respond wonderfully. Using them to preach on Wednesday night or for some other meeting at the church, to teach regularly, and to lead in general ways is an effective tool for keeping them involved in the work of the church. When there is a funeral, use a man to assist you in some way in a spiritual ministry. He learns that is his responsibility as well as that of the pastor, and he will love having the opportunity to make a difference in people's lives.

These are only a few of the ways by which you can begin to attract and keep men in your church. There are hundreds of other things that could be done also, but hopefully this will stir your minds to action and we will begin once again to reach men for Christ. Remember that in reaching men for Christ, you will reach the whole family. Our concern for where people spend eternity ought to be sufficient to spur us to do the best that we can to reach all people for Christ. Let's begin with the head of the household.

AFTERWORD

Again, there are wholesome activities other than hunting and fishing in which men may engage the young for whom they hold obligations and upon whom they may wield positive influence. We encourage participation in all such endeavors. Any wholesome activity that gets young people physically and mentally active outside and puts them into a situation where vital lessons and valuable skills may be learned represents a worthwhile undertaking.

Taking the young into the field or onto the water to hunt and fish presents an opportunity unique among all other activities. In the kind and variety of knowledge and the combination of skills that can be passed down, no single endeavor will be found as an equivalent. At a time when the minds and bodies of most of our young are being dulled and rendered effete by their absorption with and constant exposure to worlds of fantasy, frivolity, and filth via electronic media and entertainment, hunting and fishing remove them from such distractions and force their minds and bodies to move. Hunting and fishing open the doors of communication between the young and the old—the strength and passion of youth engaging the wisdom and counsel of graying heads—allowing opportunities for the teaching of the most important lessons in life. More significantly, the degree to which hunting and fishing expose all taking part, young and old, to the presence, power, and majesty of God cannot be duplicated.

Mysteries of the Bush

For Christians, hunting and fishing are—as always they have been and forever they will be—significant components of our spiritual heritage. From Nimrod, the mighty hunter before the Lord, to the covenant of Abraham, the heritage is passed on through Isaac in his love of the savory nourishment of wild game and through Ishmael who excelled in taking game with bow and arrow in the wild, silent realms of the desert. The heritage is passed down from Job, who would appear to have always been ready for a challenging hunt or fishing expedition, as well as from Benaiah, David, Solomon, and the many other adventurous souls who clearly knew the thrill, challenge, and solace of the hunt. Our heritage of fishing was set forth and given its foundational place in the enactment of our faith by Jesus Himself in His call to Peter and Andrew on the Sea of Galilee. From the call, the great catch and breakfast of roasted fish upon the same shore, and His final instructions to the disciples thereafter stems the importance of fishing as the sole allegory of the primary mandate of our faith.

To become a skilled hunter and fisherman is good and always imparts benefits and blessings to those who go afield or to the water. Yet if trophies and meat are all that is taken from the wild lands and the waters, then neither the pith nor the fullness of the potential role of either in the spirits and souls of men has been rightly understood or appreciated. To begin to understand the whole of the essence of hunting and fishing is first to realize the manifold gifts and blessings attainable thereby, which have nothing to do with shooting, casting, game, or fish.